D0423382

COLUMBUS
and the
CROWNS

COLUMBUS and the CROWNS

Edited from William H. Prescott's
History of the Reign of Ferdinand & Isabella
by David Bowen

with an Introduction by Prof. Robert W. Patch
and Illustrations by Frank W. Harris III

CORONA PUBLISHING COMPANY
San Antonio, Texas
1991

Library of Congress Catalog Card Number: 90-80855

ISBN 0-931722-82-9 (HB)
ISBN 0-931722-83-7 (pbk)

Printed and bound in the United States of America.

Cover design by Paul Hudgins. The illustration is from an engraving, ca. 1572, of the bird's-eye plan of Seville drawn by the Antwerpian painter George Hoefnagel. The houses on the near side of the Guadalquivir River are the residence of the Admiral's son, Fernando. Across the river is the monastery of Las Cuevas where Columbus was first interred.

CONTENTS

COLUMBUS
and the
CROWNS

PREFACE

For many generations of Americans, reading about history meant reading the works of William H. Prescott. Of course, this great historian was renowned well beyond the United States, and his books were eventually translated into many European languages. Nevertheless, Prescott was a very American historian, and his work represented a significant contribution not just to historiography but also to the development of American culture.

William Hickling Prescott was born in Salem, Massachusetts in 1796. His father, a successful lawyer, and mother were both descendants of the Puritan founders of New England, and the future historian was undoubtedly named for his grandfather, the William Prescott of Bunker Hill fame. Like most young men of his class, Prescott studied at Harvard. He seems to have had a career in the law in mind at first, but then an accident blinded him in one eye and rheumatism severely weakened the other. A normal professional career thus became an impossibility; indeed, his frequent total blindness would have destroyed the possibility of any career for almost anyone else. But Prescott accepted his fate with admirable good cheer, and finally discovered that his limited vision did permit him to function as a writer. Fortunately, his family had the means to support its unfortunate son in his endeavor, and he even managed to travel to England, France, and Italy in 1815-17.

After devoting himself to writing literary reviews for some years, Prescott decided at the age of twenty-six to write about history. Apparently his first thoughts were directed towards Germany, but his limited vision made it impossible for him to read original manuscripts written in the Gothic script of German. It was at first with some reluctance that he turned to Spanish history, for like most New Englanders and Englishmen, he had an instinctive dislike for Spain because of that country's religion, intolerance, obscurantism, and decadence. Nevertheless, once he had immersed himself in the subject and learned that Spaniards must be judged by their past, he developed that admiration and love for Spain which so many American, English, and French Hispanists have since come to have. Prescott's passion for his subject endured until his death.

History of the Reign of Ferdinand and Isabella, the Catholic, Prescott's first major work, was completed in 1836 and was published the following year. Like many first authors, Prescott had misgivings about publishing the work, for he was aware of its shortcomings. In fact, throughout his life he was his own most demanding critic, and was always willing to accept the well-founded criticisms of others. The arrogance of presumed perfection never entered his New England mind. Nevertheless, it was undoubtedly with some relief that he read the favorable reviews of his book, as scholars not only in the United States but also in Britain, France, and Spain took note of the new historian from the New World. He took up or continued correspondence with many of the great scholars of his day, and became determined to continue and refine his craft as historian. In 1838 Prescott turned to the topic which would make him famous beyond the confines of scholarship: the Spanish conquest of Mexico and Peru. He worked with his characteristic diligence, and in 1843 *History of the Conquest of Mexico*, his unquestioned masterpiece, was finished. This was followed, in 1846, by *History of the Conquest of Peru*, which was slightly inferior to the former only because the sources available for the study of Peru are inferior to those of Mexico. Both books were instant successes, and became the means by which educated people ever since have learned about Cortés, Pizarro, Motecuhzoma (better known, of course, as Montezuma), Atahualpa, the Aztecs, the Incas, and even Mexico and Peru.

Prescott then turned to his last, and most ambitious, project: a history of the reign of Philip II. But his eyesight by this time was so greatly deteriorated that he began to doubt whether he could in fact carry out the enormous quantity of research and writing necessary to bring the project to conclusion. Almost in despair, Prescott took a vacation, and in 1850 he journeyed once again to England. There he was treated with hospitality never shown before or since to an American scholar or intellectual. He was invited to numerous social gatherings, chatted with future Prime Minister and historian Benjamin Disraeli, and even had an audience with Queen Victoria. Prescott did not succumb to flattery, but he did take heart at the enthusiasm for his work. Overcoming his own doubts and self-criticism, Prescott returned to his work with revived spirits and renewed determination. The first volume was completed in 1852, the second in 1854, and the third was almost done in 1858 when he suffered a stroke. Deteriorating health slowed him down considerably, but he continued his work and succeeded in finishing the third volume. He even started the fourth. The project, however, would never be completed. Prescott suffered a second stroke and died on January 28, 1859.

II

In the nineteenth century, history was considered to be a branch of literature, and educated people did not always distinguish between the two. Indeed, the classics of historiography—Thucydides, Herodotus, etc.—were read as much for their literary as for their historical value. Prescott in fact was at first drawn to history because of his earlier interest in literature. But what eventually made him stand out from most people of his time was his professionalism. This was demonstrated, firstly, in his use of primary sources as the basis of his works. Of course, for a person with Prescott's physical handicaps, using archival material directly was next to impossible; manuscripts are by their very nature hard to read, and archives are usually cold, dank, and poorly lit. Prescott was able to get around these problems because members of the international scholarly community helped him by providing him with transcriptions of documents. In this respect, too, Prescott was a professional, for he communicated and made friends with other scholars, who would not have helped him had they not held him in the highest regard and considered him to be a serious historian.

Prescott's professionalism was also demonstrated by his mastery of the languages necessary for research. Like most New England gentlemen he had studied Latin and Greek as a student, but Spanish (or, more accurately stated, Castilian) was a language which he had to learn as an adult or else change his profession. With characteristic energy, Prescott accomplished his goal. With language training and the availability of archival material, he was then prepared to be not a dilettante, like so many contemporaries, but rather a professional historian.

Prescott's approach to the study of history was influenced by the times in which he lived. He was criticized by German scholars for his ostensible lack of a philosophy of history, but this is merely because Prescott, unlike the Germans, did not inform his readers from the beginning of his conception of history. In this he was clearly in the British tradition of empiricism, which in practice meant an approach emphasizing the facts rather than the laws of history. In fact, Prescott's philosophy is evident on every page he wrote. He believed, firstly, in Liberalism, that is, belief in progress and freedom, especially freedom for the individual. As a result, Prescott always praised historical developments that were progressive, such as education, science, and learning, and clearly favored any trend towards tolerance and democracy. People or institutions holding up progress and freedom—such as the Spanish Inquisition—were treated with contempt.

At the same time Prescott was clearly a product of his time because of his adherence to Romanticism. This was an ideology emphasizing the heroic in human nature, and helps account for Prescott's interest in the great men— and one great woman—in Spanish history. Nineteenth-century Romantics interpreted history as the result not of the impersonal forces of economics or social structures but of the great individuals who by their ability and will made history. These people were admired and even idolized, even though—as in the cases of Ferdinand, Columbus, and Pizarro—they were sometimes ruthless and even brutal as human beings. The Romantic philosophy often meant emphasizing the positive at the expense of the negative.

The study of history has changed remarkably since Prescott's days. The Liberal and Romantic ideologies, after all, were elitist; they excluded the masses from history, denied that anyone but the elite was important, and ignored economic factors. Focusing on the great people meant leaving all but a handful of women out of history altogether. And belief in progress really meant the progress of Western Civilization; other cultures were either ignored, or—in the case of native American civilizations—denigrated.

Since Prescott's time the study of history has changed not only because of the emergence of less chauvinistic points of view. Just as important, historiography has been transformed by the emergence of the social sciences. History has ceased to be a branch of literature, and is now considered at least partly as a social science. It employs concepts from anthropology, economics, sociology, and geography in its analysis. The great historical figures are now put into a wider context in which economic and social factors are often considered as important as, or even more important than, the great individuals.

Modern historiography has paid a price for its new conception of history: few people but professionals read it. There exists, in other words, a divorce between professional historians and the general reading public. Prescott, however, succeeded in communicating and making history interesting and relevant to everyone. This is one more measure of his greatness as a historian. This abridgement—based on Prescott's *History of the Reign of Ferdinand and Isabella*—will give people of today the opportunity to rediscover the excitement that is history and enjoy the writings of a true master on a subject of supreme relevance to the modern world. For when it comes to writing about history in a dramatic and meaningful way, no one thus far has equalled Prescott, and probably no one ever will.

III

Christopher Columbus was a man whom Prescott greatly admired. The historian could not help but be thrilled by the Italian explorer's intellectual boldness, iron will, physical courage and historical accomplishment. Columbus had everything a Romantic could want. Prescott thus treats his subject with the great respect to be paid to the truly great men of history. In this, the historian was again a man of his time, for Columbus, after being considered a failure by his contemporaries, had by the nineteenth century been elevated to the status of legend. Prescott, then, represented the culmination of a historiographical trend which had rescued Columbus from oblivion. The Italian explorer's reputation reached its zenith in the work of Prescott.

Since then, Columbus has been brought back down to human scale. The determination with which he argued his case is now seen as mere stubbornness. After all, when Columbus argued with the scientists of the University of Salamanca, he was wrong: the argument was not over whether the world was round but over its size, and the scientists were right in stating that Columbus, in miscalculating the earth's circumference, was underestimating the distance between Europe and Asia. And Columbus' insistence that he had found a new route to India despite evidence to the contrary is best understood as a manifestation of a flaw in his character: his inability to admit that he was wrong. This showed up again and again in his enterprises, the failure of which Columbus blamed on everyone and anyone but himself. And his failures were many. Columbus, bluntly stated, was lacking in the qualities of leadership. He took advice from no one, made decisions on the basis of favoritism and personal interest, and mistreated and manipulated people to accomplish his ends. He was not, as the Spaniards would have said, a good captain. Spanish colonization, which under Columbus' rule began the process of exterminating the native people of the Caribbean, would find more effective, and humane, leadership elsewhere.

But before Columbus is once more thrown into the trash heap of history, it should be noted that modern historians have also found much in him to admire. Whatever his personal defects may have been, he was a man of considerable ability. He was an excellent sailor and navigator, and a true master of the art of dead reckoning (determining longitude by estimating the distance traveled). His ships rode out a hurricane at sea on their return voyage to Spain in 1493, and his ships did this again in 1501, surviving an ordeal that sent a nearby Spanish fleet, under a less competent commander, to the bottom. When Columbus wanted to get back to the Caribbean as fast as possible in 1493, he made the crossing, on his second voyage to America, from the Canaries to the Windward Islands in only three weeks, and arrived exactly where he had intended. And Columbus was truly a master explorer. His exploration of the Caribbean was done with consummate skill, and his description of the coastline and channels is so accurate that a historian-sailor of the twentieth century was able to retrace his steps using little more than Columbus' own record as a guide. And finally, and above all else, it was Christopher Columbus who for better or worse led Europeans into what was for them a new world and thus forever changed the course of history.

Of course, what happened—or better stated, began—in 1492 has long been debated, and is being debated now, exactly five centuries later. For native Americans, Columbus' discovery of America initiated an invasion which culminated in what can only be termed a tragedy. Whole civilizations were destroyed, and entire peoples were exterminated. Survivors were either relegated to marginal and inhospitable areas called reservations, or conquered and made into peasants. As Joseph Conrad wrote later in Heart of Darkness, "The conquest of the earth . . . is not a pretty thing when you look into it too much."

But was Columbus responsible for this? Here modern

historians can lend an explanatory hand where Prescott cannot. Clearly, what happened after 1492 would have happened even if the initial discovery of America had been made by an individual with the morality of a saint. For the discovery unleashed forces in European society for which no single person—and certainly not Columbus—was responsible. The tragedy of the American Indian was truly the result of these impersonal forces associated with the expanding economy and society of Renaissance Europe. Columbus of course played his part in this tragedy, but his role in this historical process was in fact a small one. And in any case, as Prescott would have been the first to admit, history is life itself and therefore is in part tragedy.

Columbus therefore must be remembered for more than just the tragic history of the native Americans, and for more than just his failures. For who does not have defects? In fact practically every great person in history—Caesar, Frederick the Great, Napoleon, Jefferson, Churchill and Franklin Roosevelt, to name just a few—had grave character flaws that led them to mistreat their fellow human beings. But history judges people by human, not divine, standards, and greatness is not the same thing as sainthood. It is to the world of the great human beings, rather than that of the saints, that Christopher Columbus belongs.

Robert W. Patch
The University of California, Riverside

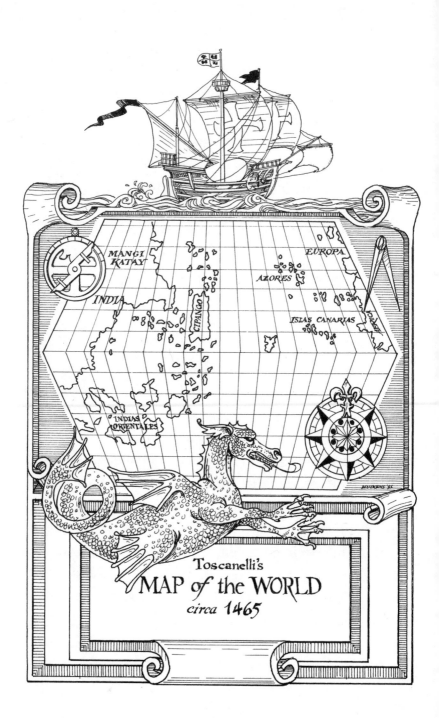

MANGI
KATAY

EUROPA

AZORES

INDIA

CIPANGO

ISLAS CANARIAS

INDIAS
ORIENTALES

Toscanelli's
MAP of the WORLD
circa 1465

INTRODUCTION

The Western Horizon

The extraordinary intellectual activity of the Europeans in the fifteenth century, after the torpor of ages, carried them forward to high advancement in almost every department of science, but especially nautical. The surprising results have acquired for that century the glory of being designated as peculiarly the age of maritime discovery. The political condition of Europe was eminently favorable to this activity. Under the Roman empire, the traffic with the east naturally centered in Rome, the commercial capital of the west. After the dismemberment of the empire, it continued to be conducted principally through the Italian ports, from which it was diffused over the remoter regions of Christendom. But these countries of western Europe, which had now risen from the rank of subordinate provinces to that of separate independent states, viewed with jealousy the monopoly of the Italian cities.

This was especially the case with Portugal and Castile, which, placed on the remote frontiers of the European continent, were far removed from the great routes of Asiatic commerce. These two nations were naturally led to turn their eyes on the great ocean which washed their western borders. They would seek in the hitherto unexplored recesses of the Atlantic for new domains—and if possible find out some undiscovered track towards the opulent regions of the east.

The spirit of maritime enterprise was greatly facilitated by the invention of the astrolabe, and the important discovery of the polarity of the magnet, whose application to the device known as the compass was widely diffused in the fifteenth century. The Portuguese were the first to enter on the brilliant path of nautical discovery. Under Prince Don Henry they pursued it with such activity that, before the middle of the fifteenth century, they had penetrated as far as Cape Verde, doubling many a fearful headland which had shut in the timid navigator of former days. At length, in 1486, they descried the lofty promontory which terminates Africa on the south. King John the Second, under whom it was discovered, hailed it as the harbinger of the long-sought passage to the east, and named it the Cape of Good Hope.

The Spaniards, in the meanwhile, did not languish in the career of maritime enterprise. Certain adventurers from the northern provinces of Biscay and Guipuscoa, in 1393, had made themselves masters of one of the smallest of the group of islands, supposed to be the Fortunate Isles of the ancients and since known as the Canaries. Other private adventurers from Seville extended their conquests over these islands in the beginning of the following century. These were completed in behalf of the crown under Ferdinand and Isabella, with the taking of Teneriffe in 1495.

From the commencement of their reign, the monarchs of Castile had shown an earnest solicitude for the encouragement of commerce and nautical science. Under them—and indeed under their predecessors as far back as Henry the Third—a considerable traffic had been carried on with the western coast of Africa, from which gold dust and slaves were imported into the city of Seville. (Isabella repeatedly interfered on behalf of these unfortunate beings, by ordinances tending to secure them a more equal protection of the laws.)

A misunderstanding gradually arose between the subjects of Castile and Portugal, in relation to their respective rights of discovery and commerce on the African coast. This promised a fruitful source of collision between the two crowns, but was happily adjusted by an article in the treaty of 1479, that terminated the War of the Succession. By this it was settled, that the right of traffic and of discovery on the western coast of Africa should be exclusively reserved to the Portuguese; they in their turn should resign all claims on the Canaries to the crown of Castile.

The Spaniards, thus excluded from further progress to the south, seemed to have no other opening left for naval adventure than the untravelled regions of the great western ocean. Fortunately, at this moment, an individual appeared among them, in the person of Christopher Columbus, endowed with capacity for stimulating them to this heroic enterprise, and conducting it to a glorious conclusion.

This extraordinary man was a native of Genoa, of humble parentage, though perhaps honorable descent. (It is very generally agreed that the father of Columbus exercised the craft of a wool-carder, or weaver. The admiral's son Ferdinand, after some speculation on the genealogy of his illustrious parent, concludes with remarking that, after all, a noble descent would confer less luster on him than to have sprung from such a father; a philosophical sentiment, indicating pretty strongly that he had no great ancestry to boast of.) He was instructed in his early youth at Pavia, where he acquired a taste for the mathematical sciences.

At the age of fourteen, he engaged in a seafaring life, which he followed with little intermission until 1470. In that year, probably little more than thirty years of age, he landed in Portugal, that great theater of maritime enterprise which attracted adventurous spirits from all parts of the world. After his arrival, he continued to make voyages to the then known parts of the world. On shore, he occupied himself with the construction and sale of charts and maps. His researches were considerably aided by the possession of papers belonging to an eminent Portuguese navigator, a deceased relative of his wife.

Thus stored with all that nautical science in that day could supply, and fortified by large practical experience, the reflecting mind of Columbus was naturally led to speculate on the existence of some other land beyond the western waters. He conceived the possibility of reaching the eastern shores of Asia—whose provinces of Cipango [Japan] and Cathay [China] were emblazoned in such gorgeous colors in the narratives of Mandeville* and others—by a more direct route than that which traversed the continent of Asia.

---

* The *Travels*, written by one who called himself "Sir John Mandeville," were published between 1357 and 1371. These colorful (and partly imaginary) narratives achieved great popularity throughout Europe. [Editor.]

-1-

The Jewels of Isabella

The existence of land beyond the Atlantic was hinted at by some of the most enlightened ancients. By the close of the fifteenth century, it had become a matter of common speculation. Maritime adventure was daily disclosing the mysteries of the deep, and bringing to light new regions that had hitherto existed only in fancy.

Columbus' hypothesis rested on much firmer ground than popular belief or learned speculation. It amounted in his mind to a settled practical conviction, that made him ready to peril life and fortune on the result of the experiment. He was fortified still further in his conclusions by a correspondence with the learned Italian Toscanelli, who furnished him with a map of his own projection, in which the eastern coast of Asia was shown opposite to the western frontier of Europe.*

Ferdinand Columbus enumerates three grounds on which his father's conviction of land in the west was founded. First, natural reason—or conclusions drawn from science; secondly, authority of writers—amounting to little more than vague speculations of the ancients; thirdly, testimony of sailors, comprehending, in addition to popular rumors of land described in western voyages, such relics as appeared to have floated to the European shores from the other side of the Atlantic.

Filled with lofty anticipations of achieving a momentous discovery, Columbus submitted his theory of a western route to King John the Second, of Portugal. Here he encountered for the first time the embarrassments and mortifications which so often obstruct the conceptions of genius, too sublime for the age in which they are formed. After a long and fruitless negotiation (and a dishonorable attempt on the part of the Portuguese to use his information in secret) he quitted Lisbon in disgust, and decided to submit his proposals to the Spanish sovereigns, relying on their reputation for wisdom and enterprise.

The period of his arrival in Spain, being the latter part of 1484, would seem to have been most unpromising.

---

* Columbus visited Iceland in 1477 and might well have learned of the Scandinavian voyages to the northern shores of America in the tenth and following centuries. But if he did, why did he not use this information in support of his own hypothesis of the existence of land in the west? And why should he have taken a route so different from that of his predecessors in the path of discovery? Perhaps the information he gathered in Iceland was too vague to suggest that these western lands had any connection with the Indies which he sought. In Columbus' day, indeed, so little was understood of the true position of these countries that Greenland is laid down on the maps as an extension of Scandinavia.

The nation was then in the heat of the Moorish war, and the sovereigns were continuously engaged in prosecuting their campaigns, or in active preparation for them. The large expenditures of the war exhausted their resources, and left them little leisure for indulging in dreams of distant and doubtful discovery.

Columbus, moreover, was unfortunate in his first channel of communication with the court. He was furnished by Fray Juan Pérez de Marchena, guardian of the convent of La Rábida in Andalusia, who had early taken a deep interest in his plans, with an introduction to Fernando de Talavera, prior of Prado. Talavera was confessor of the queen, a person high in the royal confidence, and recently become the archbishop of Granada. He was a man of irreproachable morals and great benevolence. He was also learned; but his learning was that of the cloister, deeply colored by pedantry and superstition, and so deferential to the errors of antiquity that he was blind to everything like innovation or enterprise.

Talavera was so far from comprehending the vast conceptions of Columbus that he seems to have regarded him as a mere visionary, and possibly worse. Ferdinand and Isabella sought the opinion of the most competent judges on the merits of Columbus' theory by referring him to a council of scholars—a council selected by Talavera. Such was the apathy of this learned conclave, and so numerous the impediments suggested by dullness, prejudice, or skepticism, that years glided away before it came to a decision. During this time, Columbus appears to have remained in attendance on the court. He bore arms occasionally in the campaigns, and was obviously well regarded by the king and queen.

At length, Columbus pressed the court for a definite answer to his propositions. He was informed that Talavera's council pronounced his scheme to be "vain, impracticable, and resting on grounds too weak to merit the support of the government."

Many in the council, however, disagreed. In fact, some of the most important persons of the court not only cordially embraced his scheme, but extended their personal intimacy and friendship to him. Such, among others, were the grand cardinal Mendoza, and also a Dominican friar named Deza, who was besides archbishop of Seville. In any event, the sovereigns softened the verdict of the junto, by an assurance to Columbus that, "although they were too much occupied at present to embark in his undertaking, yet, at the conclusion of the war, they should find both time and inclination to treat with him."

Far from welcoming the qualified assurance of the sovereigns, Columbus seems to have considered their refusal as peremptory and final. In great dejection of mind, therefore, he quitted the court, with the intent of seeking out some other patron to his undertaking.

Columbus had already visited his native city of Genoa, for the purpose of interesting it in his scheme of discovery; but the attempt proved unsuccessful. He made application to the dukes of Medina Sidonia and Medina Celi, successively. From the latter he experienced much kindness and hospitality; but neither of these nobles, whose large estates lying along the seashore had often invited them to maritime adventure, was disposed to assume one which seemed too hazardous for the resources of the crown. Without wasting time in further solicitation, Columbus prepared with a heavy heart to bid adieu to Spain, and carry his proposals to the king of France, from whom he had received a letter of encouragement while detained in Andalusia.

While at the convent of La Rábida (which he visited previous to his departure), he was persuaded by his friend, Juan Pérez, the guardian of the convent, to postpone his journey till another effort had been made to move the Spanish court in his favor. For this purpose the worthy ecclesiastic undertook an expedition in person to the newly erected city of Santa Fe, where the sovereigns lay encamped before Granada. Juan Pérez had formerly been confessor of Isabella, and was held in great esteem by her. On arriving at the camp, he was readily admitted to an audience, and he pressed the suit of Columbus with all the earnestness and reasoning of which he was capable.

The friar's eloquence was supported by that of several eminent persons, whom Columbus during his long residence in the country had interested in his project. Among these individuals are particularly mentioned

Alonso de Quintanilla, comptroller general of Castile, Louis de San Angel, a fiscal officer of the crown of Aragon, and the marchioness of Moya, the personal friend of Isabella. Their considerable influence, coming at a moment when the approaching termination of the Moorish war allowed room for interest in other objects, encouraged the sovereigns to resume the negotiation with Columbus. An invitation was accordingly sent to him to come to Santa Fe, and a considerable sum was provided for his equipment and his expenses on the road.

Columbus lost no time in responding to this welcome news and arrived at the camp in time to witness the surrender of Granada. Every heart, swelling with exultation at the triumphant termination of the war, was naturally disposed to enter with confidence upon new adventures. At his interview with the king and queen, he once more exhibited the arguments on which his hypothesis was founded. He did not hesitate to stimulate the greed of his audience by picturing the realms of Mangi and Cathay—which he confidently expected to reach by this western route—in all the barbaric splendors which had been shed over them by the lively fancy of Marco Polo and other travellers of the Middle Ages.

He concluded by appealing to a higher principle: holding out the prospect of extending the empire of the Cross over nations of benighted heathen, while he proposed to devote the profits of his enterprise to the recovery of the Holy Sepulcher. (This last might well have passed for fanaticism in a later day, and given a visionary tinge to his whole project. But it was not quite so preposterous in an age in which the spirit of the crusades might be said still to linger, and the romance of religion had not yet been dispelled by sober reason.) The more temperate suggestion of the diffusion of the gospel was well suited to affect the devout Isabella. She, in all her undertakings, seems to have been far less open to the vulgar impulses of avarice or ambition, than to any argument connected with the interests of religion.

An obstacle unexpectedly arose when Columbus stipulated for himself and heirs the title and authority of Admiral and Viceroy over all lands discovered by him, with one-tenth of the profits. This was deemed wholly inadmissible. Ferdinand, who had looked with cold distrust on the expedition from the first, was supported by Talavera, the new archbishop of Granada, who declared, that "such demands savored of the highest degree of arrogance, and would be unbecoming in their Highnesses to grant to a needy foreign adventurer." Columbus, however, steadily resisted every attempt to induce him to modify his propositions. On this ground, the conferences were abruptly broken off, and he once more turned his back upon the Spanish court. He was resolved rather to forego his splendid anticipations of discovery than surrender one of the honorable distinctions due to his services. This last act is perhaps the most remarkable exhibition in his whole life of that proud, unyielding spirit, which sustained him through so many years of trial and enabled him at length to achieve his great enterprise, in the face of every obstacle which man and nature had opposed to it.

The misunderstanding was not of long duration. Columbus' friends, and especially Louis de San Angel, remonstrated with the queen in the most earnest manner. He frankly told her that Columbus' demands, if high, were at least contingent on success, when they would be well deserved; if he failed, he required nothing. He praised Columbus' qualifications for the undertaking, and pointed out that they might attract the patronage of some other monarch, who would reap the fruits of his discoveries. San Angel also ventured to remind the queen that her present policy was not in accordance with the magnanimous spirit which had made her the ready patron of great and heroic enterprise.

Isabella was moved by this honest eloquence. Refusing to listen any longer to her cold and timid counsellors, she gave way to the natural impulses of her own noble and generous heart. "I will assume the undertaking," said she, "for my own crown of Castile, and am ready to pawn my jewels to defray the expenses of it, if the funds in the treasury shall be found inadequate." The treasury had been reduced to the lowest ebb by the late war, but the receiver, San Angel, advanced the required sums from the Aragonese revenues deposited in his hands. Aragon, however, was not considered as adventuring in the expedition, the charges and the profits of which were reserved exclusively for Castile.

Columbus was overtaken by the royal messenger at only a few leagues' distance from Granada. He found the most courteous reception on his return to Santa Fe and a definitive arrangement was concluded with the Spanish sovereigns on April 17th, 1492. By its terms, Ferdinand and Isabella, as lords of the ocean-seas, constituted Christopher Columbus their admiral, viceroy, and governor-general of all such islands and continents as he should discover in the western ocean. Further, he would have the privilege of nominating three candidates, for the selection of one by the crown, for the government of each of these territories. He was to be vested with exclusive right of jurisdiction over all commercial transactions within his admiralty. He was to be entitled to one-tenth of all the products and profits within the limits of his discoveries, and an additional eighth, provided he should contribute one-eighth part of the expense. By a subsequent ordinance, the official titles above enumerated were settled on him and his heirs for ever, with the privilege of prefixing to their names the title of Don (which had not then degenerated into an appellation of mere courtesy).

No sooner were the arrangements completed, than Isabella prepared with her characteristic promptness to forward the expedition. Orders were sent to Seville and the other ports of Andalusia, to furnish stores and other articles needed for the voyage, free of duty, and at as low

Portion of a contract or *capitulación* between
Columbus and the Spanish sovereigns. Like all such
documents, it begins with the full titles of Isabella
and Ferdinand:

*Don Ferdinand and Donna Isabel, by the grace of God
King and Queen of Castile, Leon, Aragon, Sicily,
Granada, Toledo, Valencia, Galicia, Majorca, Seville,
Sardinia, Cordova, Corsica, Murcia, Jaen, the
Algarves, Algeciras, Gibraltar, and the Canary
Islands, Count and Countess of Barcelona, Lords of
Biscay and Molina, Dukes of Athens and Neopatria,
Counts of Roussillon and Cerdagne, Marquises of
Oristano and Goziano.*

rates as possible. The fleet, consisting of three vessels, was to sail from the little port of Palos in Andalusia, which had been condemned for some delinquency to maintain two caravels for a twelvemonth for the public service. The third vessel was furnished by the admiral. In this he appears to have been aided by his friend the guardian of La Rábida, and the Pinzons, a family in Palos long distinguished for its enterprise among the mariners of that active community.

In less than three months the little squadron was equipped for sea, despite the open opposition of many Andalusian mariners to the perilous voyage. Sufficient evidence of the extreme unpopularity of the expedition is a royal ordinance of the 30th of April, promising protection to all persons who should embark in it, from criminal prosecution of whatever kind, until two months after their return.

The armament consisted of two caravels (light vessels without decks) and a third of larger burden. The total number of persons who embarked amounted to one hundred and twenty; and the whole charges of the crown for the expedition did not exceed seventeen thousand florins. The fleet was instructed to keep clear of the African coast, and other maritime possessions of Portugal.

At length, all things being in readiness, Columbus and his whole crew partook of the sacrament, and confessed themselves. On the morning of the 3rd of August, 1492, the intrepid navigator, bidding adieu to the Old

World, launched forth on that unfathomed waste of waters where no sail had ever been spread before.

It is impossible to peruse the story of Columbus without assigning to him almost exclusively the glory of his great discovery; for, from the first moment of its conception to that of its final execution, he encountered every kind of mortification and embarrassment, with scarcely a heart to cheer, or a hand to help him. Even those more enlightened persons whom he succeeded in interesting in his expedition, looked upon it with only a vague and skeptical curiosity. Very little mention is made of it in the correspondence and other writings of that time, previous to the actual discovery. Peter Martyr, one of the most accomplished scholars of the period, had long resided at the Castilian court and must have been fully aware of the designs of Columbus. Though he later took the deepest interest in the results of Columbus' discoveries, he does not, so far as I am aware, allude to him in his voluminous correspondence with the learned men of his time, previous to the first expedition. The common people regarded, not merely with apathy but with terror, the prospect of a voyage on the boundless wilderness of waters, which tradition and superstitious fancy had peopled with innumerable horrors.

It is true that Columbus experienced a most honorable reception at the Castilian court, such as naturally flowed from the benevolent spirit of Isabella. But the queen was too little proficient in science to be able to estimate the merits of his hypothesis. Since many of those on whose judgment she leaned, regarded it as fanciful, it is unlikely that she entertained a deep conviction of its truth. Certainly it did not attract the generous expenditure which she readily supplied to schemes of real importance. The paltry amount actually expended on Columbus' first expedition was far less than the cost of a fleet of similar size embarked in the recent Moorish war, and less than the Queen was willing to spend in the ensuing year, after Columbus' discoveries.

But we must remember, in justice to Isabella, that, although tardily, she did in fact furnish the resources essential to Columbus' undertaking; that she undertook the enterprise when it had been explicitly declined by other powers; and that, after once pledging her faith to Columbus, she became his steady friend, shielding him against his enemies and supplying ample resources for the prosecution of his glorious discoveries.

Columbus, in a letter written on his third voyage, pays heartfelt tribute to the patronage which he experienced from the queen. "In the midst of the general incredulity," says he, "the Almighty infused into the queen, my lady, the spirit of intelligence and energy; and, whilst every one else, in his ignorance, was expatiating only on the inconvenience and cost, her Highness approved it, on the contrary, and gave it all the support in her power."

-2-

The Pope and the Portuguese

As is well known, the great navigator had succeeded—after a voyage whose natural difficulties were much augmented by the distrust and mutinous spirit of his followers—in descrying land on Friday, the 12th of October, 1492. After some months spent in exploring the delightful regions, now for the first time thrown open to the eyes of a European, he embarked in the month of January, 1493, for Spain. One of his vessels had previously foundered, and another had deserted him; so that he was left alone to retrace his course across the Atlantic.

After a most tempestuous voyage, he was compelled to take shelter in the Tagus River in Portugal, much against his inclination. According to the chronicle of one Ruy de Pina [1790-93], the Portuguese monarch John the

Second found Columbus to be "overbearing and puffed up by his success," and there were those who urged that he be killed on the spot. His death, it was thought, would put an end to the Spanish undertaking and could easily be made to appear the result of his own indiscretion. Yet the king, "as he was a prince greatly fearing God, not only forbade this, but even showed the admiral honor and much favor, and therewith dismissed him."

After a brief delay, the admiral resumed his voyage, and entered the harbor of Palos about noon, on the 15th of March, 1493. It was exactly seven months and eleven days since his departure from that port.

Great was the agitation in the little community of Palos, as they beheld the well-known vessel of the admiral reentering their harbor. Their desponding imaginations had long since consigned him to a watery grave; for, in addition to the preternatural horrors which hung over the voyage, they had experienced the most stormy and disastrous winter within the recollection of the oldest mariners. Most of them had relatives or friends on board. They thronged immediately to the shore, to assure themselves with their own eyes of the truth of their return.

The whole population of the place accompanied Columbus and his crew to the principal church, where solemn thanksgivings were offered up for their return; every bell in the village sent forth a joyous peal in honor of the glorious event.

In this spring of 1493, the Spanish court was still at

34

Barcelona. It was here that letters were received from Christopher Columbus, announcing his return to Spain, and the successful discovery of land beyond the western ocean. The delight and astonishment raised by this intelligence were as great as the skepticism with which his project had been originally viewed. The sovereigns were now filled with a natural impatience to learn the extent and other particulars of the important discovery. They transmitted instant instructions to the admiral to come to Barcelona, as soon as he could complete arrangements for the further prosecution of his enterprise.

The admiral was too desirous of presenting himself before the sovereigns, to protract his stay long at Palos. He took with him on his journey specimens of the products of the newly discovered regions. He was accompanied by several of the native islanders, arrayed in their simple barbaric costume, and decorated, as he passed through the principal cities, with collars, bracelets, and other ornaments of gold, rudely fashioned. He exhibited also considerable quantities of the same metal in dust, or in crude masses, numerous exotic vegetables, possessed of aromatic or medicinal virtue, several kinds of quadrupeds unknown in Europe, and birds whose varieties of gaudy plumage gave a brilliant effect to the pageant.

The admiral's progress through the country was everywhere impeded by the multitudes thronging forth to gaze at the extraordinary spectacle, and the more extraordinary man, who, in the emphatic language of that time (which has now lost its force from its familiarity) first revealed the existence of a "New World." As he passed through the busy, populous city of Seville, every window, balcony, and housetop, which could afford a glimpse of him, was crowded with spectators.

It was the middle of April before Columbus reached Barcelona. The nobility and cavaliers in attendance on the court, together with the authorities of the city, came to the gates to receive him, and escorted him to the royal presence. Ferdinand and Isabella were seated, with their son, Prince John, under a superb canopy of state, awaiting his arrival. On his approach, they rose from their seats, and, extending their hands to him, caused him to be seated before them. These were unprecedented marks of condescension to a person of Columbus's rank, in the haughty and ceremonious court of Castile.

It was, indeed, the proudest moment in the life of Columbus. He had fully established the truth of his long-contested theory, in the face of argument, sophistry, sneer, skepticism, and contempt. The honors paid him—hitherto reserved only for rank, or fortune, or military success, purchased by the blood and tears of thousands—were, in his case, a homage to intellectual power, successfully exerted in behalf of the noblest interests of humanity.

When the sovereigns requested from Columbus a recital of his adventures, he replied in a manner that was sedate and dignified, but warmed by the glow of natural enthusiasm. He enumerated the several islands which he had visited, praised the temperate character of the climate, and the capacity of the soil for every variety of agricultural production, displaying the samples imported by him, as evidence of their natural fruitfulness. He spoke at length of the precious metals to be found in these islands (inferred less from the specimens actually obtained than from the uniform testimony of the natives). Lastly, he pointed out the wide scope for Christian zeal, in the illumination of a race of men, whose minds were not wedded to any system of idolatry, but were prepared by their extreme simplicity for the reception of pure and uncorrupted doctrine. The last consideration touched Isabella's heart most sensibly; and the whole audience, kindled with various emotions by the speaker's eloquence, filled up the perspective with the gorgeous coloring of their own fancies, as ambition, or avarice, or devotional feeling predominated in their bosoms. When Columbus ceased, the king and queen, together with all present, prostrated themselves on their knees in grateful thanksgivings, while the solemn strains of the Te Deum were poured forth by the choir of the royal chapel, as in commemoration of some glorious victory.

The discoveries of Columbus excited a sensation, particularly among men of science, in the most distant parts of Europe. They congratulated one another on living in an age which had witnessed so grand an event. The learned Peter Martyr (who, in his wide correspondence, had not even deigned to notice the preparations for the voyage of discovery) now lavished unbounded praise on its results. Most of the scholars of the day, however, adopted the erroneous hypothesis of Columbus, who considered the lands he had discovered as bordering on the eastern shores of Asia. This view was supported by the apparent similarity between various natural products of these islands, and of the east. From this error, the new dominions soon came to be distinguished as the "West Indies," an appellation by which they are still recognized in the titles of the Spanish crown.

Columbus, during his residence at Barcelona, continued to receive from the Spanish sovereigns the most honorable distinctions which royal bounty could confer. When King Ferdinand rode abroad, he was accompanied by the admiral at his side. The courtiers, too, made frequent entertainments, at which he was treated with the deference paid to a noble of the highest class. He was permitted to quarter the royal arms with his own, which consisted of a group of golden islands amid azure billows. He received besides, soon after his return, the substantial gratuity of a thousand *doblas* of gold, from the royal treasury, and the premium of 10,000 *maravédies*, promised to the person who first descried land.

But the attentions most welcome to his lofty spirit were the preparations of the Spanish court for prosecuting his discoveries, on a scale worthy of their importance. A board was established for the direction of Indian affairs, consisting of a superintendent and two subordinates. The first of these officers was Juan de Fonseca, archdeacon of Seville, an active, ambitious prelate, whose shrewdness and capacity for business enabled him to maintain the control of the Indian department during the whole of the present reign. An office for the transaction of business was instituted at Seville, and a custom-house placed under its direction at Cádiz. This was the origin of the important establishment of the *Casa de la Contratación de las Indias*, or India House.

The commercial regulations adopted exhibit a narrow policy typical of the age. The new territories, far from being permitted free intercourse with foreign nations, were opened only to Spanish subjects, and were reserved as part of the exclusive revenue of the crown. All persons of whatever description were prohibited, under the severest penalties, from trading with, or even visiting the Indies, without license from the constituted authorities. It was impossible to evade this, as a minute specification of the ships, cargoes, and crews, with the property belonging to each individual, was required to be taken at the office in Cádiz. A corresponding registration was made in a similar office established at Hispaniola in the Indies.

A wiser spirit was shown in the ample provision of whatever could contribute to the support or permanent prosperity of the infant colony. Grain, plants, the seeds of numerous vegetable products—which in the genial climate of the Indies might be made valuable articles for domestic consumption or export—were liberally furnished. Commodities for the supply of the fleet were exempted from duty. The owners of all vessels throughout the ports of Andalusia were required (by an ordinance somewhat arbitrary) to hold them in readiness for the expedition. Still further authority was given to impress both officers and men, if necessary, into the service. Artisans of every sort, provided with the implements of their various crafts, including a great number of miners for exploring the subterranean treasures of the new regions, were enrolled in the expedition. In order to defray the heavy charges of all this, the government, in addition to its regular resources, had recourse to a loan, and to the confiscated property of the recently exiled Jews.

Amid their own temporal concerns, the Spanish sovereigns did not forget the spiritual interests of their new subjects. The Indians, who accompanied Columbus to Barcelona, had been all of them baptized. King Ferdinand, and his son, Prince John, stood as sponsors to two of them, who were permitted to take their names. One of the Indians remained attached to the prince's establishment; the residue was sent to Seville, where after suitable religious instruction, they were to be returned as missionaries for the propagation of the faith among their own countrymen. Twelve Spanish ecclesiastics were also destined to this service; among whom was the celebrated Las Casas, so conspicuous afterwards for his benevolent exertions in behalf of the unfortunate natives.

The most explicit directions were given to the admiral, to use every effort for the illumination of the poor heathen, which was set forth as the primary object of the expedition. He was particularly enjoined "to abstain from all means of annoyance, and to treat them well and lovingly, maintaining a familiar intercourse with them, rendering them all the kind offices in his power, distributing presents of the merchandise and various commodities, which their Highnesses had caused to be embarked on board the fleet for that purpose; and finally, to chastise, in the most exemplary manner, all who should offer the natives the slightest molestation." The indulgent tenor of these instructions attests to the benevolent and rational views of Isabella in religious matters, when not warped by any foreign influence.

Towards the last of May, Columbus quitted Barcelona for the purpose of superintending the preparations for departure on his second voyage. He was accompanied to the gates of the city by all the nobility and cavaliers of the court. Orders were issued to the different towns to provide him and his suite with lodgings free of expense. His former commission was not only confirmed in its full extent, but considerably enlarged. He was authorized to nominate to all offices, without application to government. Ordinances and letters patent, bearing the royal seal, were to be issued by him, subscribed by himself or his deputy. However tardy the sovereigns may have been in granting him their confidence, they were clearly not disposed to stint the measure of it now.

Soon after Columbus' return to Spain, Ferdinand and Isabella applied to the court of Rome, to confirm them in the possession of their recent discoveries, and invest them with similar jurisdiction to that formerly conferred on the kings of Portugal. It was an opinion—as ancient perhaps as the crusades—that the pope, as vicar of Christ, had competent authority to dispose of all countries inhabited by heathen nations, in favor of Christian potentates. Although Ferdinand and Isabella do not seem to have been fully satisfied of this right, yet they were willing to make use of it in the present instance. The papal sanction would most effectually exclude the pretensions of all others, and especially their Portuguese rivals.

The pontifical throne was at that time filled by Alexander the Sixth. Although degraded by the most sordid appetites, he was endowed by nature with singular acuteness, as well as energy of character. He lent a willing ear to the application of the Spanish government, and made no hesitation in granting what cost him nothing, while it recognized the assumption of powers which had already begun to totter in the opinion of mankind.

On the 3rd of May, 1493, Pope Alexander published a bull, in which, taking into consideration the eminent services of the Spanish monarchs in the cause of the church (especially in the subversion of the Mahometan empire in Spain), he moved to afford then still wider scope for their pious labors. To this end, he confirmed them in the possession of all lands discovered or hereafter to be discovered by them in the western ocean.

This bull he supported by another, dated on the following day. In it the pope, in order to avoid any misunderstanding with the Portuguese (and acting no doubt on the suggestion of the Spanish sovereigns) defined with greater precision his original grant to the latter. He bestowed on them all such lands as they should discover to the west of an imaginary line, to be drawn from pole to pole, at the distance of one hundred leagues to the west of the Azores and Cape Verde Islands.

It seems to have escaped his Holiness, that the Spaniards, by pursuing a western route, might in time reach the eastern limits of countries previously granted to the Portuguese. At least this would appear from the import of a third bull, issued September 25th of the same year, which invested the sovereigns with plenary authority over all countries discovered by them, whether in the east, or within the boundaries of India, all previous concessions to the contrary notwithstanding. With the title derived from actual possession, and fortified by the highest ecclesiastical sanction, the Spaniards foresaw an uninterrupted career of discovery. They did not reckon, however, with the jealousy of their rivals, the Portuguese.

The court of Lisbon viewed with secret disquietude the increasing maritime enterprise of its neighbors. While the Portuguese were timidly creeping along the barren shores of Africa, the Spaniards had boldly launched into the deep, and encountered realms which teemed in their fancies with inestimable wealth. The Portuguese could not but reflect that all this might have been achieved for themselves, had they known how to profit by the proposals of Columbus. From the first moment in which the success of the admiral's enterprise was established, John the Second, a politic and ambitious prince, had sought some pretense to check the career of discovery, or at least to share in the spoils of it.

In his interview with Columbus, at Lisbon, he suggested that the discoveries of the Spaniards might interfere with the rights secured to the Portuguese by repeated papal sanctions since the beginning of the 15th century, and guaranteed by the treaty with Spain in 1479. Columbus, without entering into the discussion, contented himself with declaring that he had been instructed by his own government to steer clear of all Portuguese settlements on the African coast, and that his course indeed had led him in an entirely different direction.

In the meanwhile, Ferdinand and Isabella received intelligence that King John was equipping a considerable armament in order to anticipate or defeat their discoveries in the west. They instantly sent one of their household, Don Lope de Herrera, as ambassador to Lisbon. His instructions were to make acknowledgment to the king for his hospitable reception of Columbus, accompanied with a request that he would prohibit his subjects from interference with the discoveries of the Spaniards in the west, in the same manner as these latter had been excluded from the Portuguese possessions in Africa.

The ambassador was furnished with orders of a different import, in case he should find the reports correct respecting the equipment and probable destination of a Portuguese armada. Instead of a conciliatory deportment, he was, in that case, to assume a tone of remonstrance, and to demand a full explanation from King John, of his designs. The cautious prince, who had received, through his secret agents in Castile, intelligence of these latter instructions, managed matters so discreetly as to give no occasion for their exercise. He abandoned, or at least postponed, his expedition, in the hope of adjusting the dispute by negotiation, in which he excelled. In order to quiet the apprehensions of the Spanish court, he engaged to fit out no fleet from his dominions within sixty days. At the same time he sent a fresh mission to Barcelona, with directions to propose an amicable adjustment of the conflicting claims of the two nations, by making the parallel of the Canaries a line of partition between them. The right of discovery to the north would be reserved to the Spaniards, and that to the south to the Portuguese.

While this game of diplomacy was going on, the Castilian court availed itself of the interval afforded by its rival, to expedite preparations for a second voyage of discovery by Columbus. These were fully completed before the close of September. Instead of the reluctance, and indeed avowed disgust, which had been manifested by all classes to his former voyage, the only embarrassment now arose from the difficulty of selecting among the multitude who pressed to be enrolled in the present expedition. The reports and speculations of the first adventurers had inflamed the greed of many. This was still further heightened by the exhibition of the rich and curious products which Columbus had brought back with him, and by the popular belief that the new discoveries formed part of that gorgeous east, "whose caverns teem with diamond flaming, and with seeds of gold," and which tradition and romance had invested with the supernatural splendors of enchantment. Many others were stimulated by the wild love of adventure, kindled in the long Moorish war, but which, now excluded from that career, sought other objects in the vast, untravelled regions of the New World.

The complement of the fleet was originally fixed at twelve hundred souls, but this was eventually swelled to fifteen hundred. Among these were many who enlisted without compensation, including several persons of rank, hidalgos, and members of the royal household. The whole squadron amounted to seventeen vessels, three of them of one hundred tons' burden each. With this gallant navy, Columbus, dropping down the Guadalquivir, took his departure from the bay of Cádiz, on the 25th of September, 1493. It was a striking contrast to the melancholy plight in which, but the year previous, he sallied forth like some forlorn knight-errant, on a desperate and chimerical enterprise.

No sooner had the fleet weighed anchor, than Ferdinand and Isabella despatched an embassy in solemn state to advise the king of Portugal of it. This embassy was composed of two persons of distinguished rank, Don Pedro de Ayala, and Don Garci López de Carbajal. They represented to the Portuguese monarch the inadmissibility of his propositions respecting the boundary line of navigation. They argued that the grants of the Holy See, and the treaty with Spain in 1479, had reference merely to the actual possessions of Portugal, and the right of discovery by an eastern route along the coasts of Africa to the Indies; that these rights had been invariably respected by Spain; that the late voyage of Columbus struck into a directly opposite track; and that the several bulls of Pope Alexander the Sixth—prescribing the line of partition, not from east to west, but from the north to the south pole— were intended to secure to the Spaniards the exclusive right of discovery in the western ocean. The ambassadors concluded with offering, in the name of their sovereigns, to refer the whole matter in dispute to the arbitration of the court of Rome, or of any common umpire.

King John was deeply chagrined at learning of the departure of the Spanish expedition. He saw that his rivals had been acting while he had been amused with negotiation. He at first threw out hints of an immediate rupture and endeavored to intimidate the Castilian ambassadors by bringing them, accidentally, as it were, in the presence of a splendid array of cavalry, mounted and ready for immediate service. He vented his spleen on the embassy, by declaring that "it was a mere abortion; having neither head nor feet"; (alluding to the personal infirmity of Ayala, who was lame, and to the light, frivolous character of the other envoy).

These symptoms of discontent were duly notified to the Spanish government. It was decided to keep a vigilant eye on the movements of the Portuguese, and, in case any hostile armament should quit their ports, to be in readiness to act against it with one double its force. King John, however, was too shrewd a prince to be drawn into war with a powerful adversary. Neither did he relish the suggestion of deciding the dispute by arbitration; he well knew that his claim rested on too unsound a basis to expect a favorable award from any impartial umpire. He had already failed in an application for redress to the court of Rome, which answered him by reference to its bulls, recently published.

In this emergency, he came to the resolution at last (which should have been first adopted) of deciding the matter by a fair and open conference. It was not until the following year, however, that commissioners named by the two crowns convened at Tordesillas, and on the 7th of June, 1494, subscribed articles of agreement, which were shortly ratified by the respective powers. In this treaty, the Spaniards were secured in the exclusive right of navigation and discovery in the western ocean. The Portuguese, however, complained that the papal line of demarcation cooped up their enterprises within too narrow limits. So it was agreed that instead of one hundred, it should be removed three hundred and seventy leagues west of the Cape Verde islands, beyond which all discoveries should appertain to the Spanish nation.

The removal of the partition line was followed by important consequences to the Portuguese, who derived from it their pretensions to the noble empire of Brazil.

Thus this singular misunderstanding, which menaced an open rupture at one time, was happily adjusted. Fortunately, the accomplishment of the passage round the Cape of Good Hope, which occurred soon afterwards, led the Portuguese in an opposite direction to their Spanish rivals, their Brazilian possessions having too little attractions, at first, to turn them from the splendid path of discovery thrown open in the east.

-3-

Columbus in Chains

In less than two years from the commencement of Columbus' second voyage, the tone of excitement in Europe experienced a melancholy change. Accounts were received of the most alarming discontent and disaffection in the colony. At the same time, the actual returns from these vaunted regions were so scanty as to bear no proportion to the expenses of the expedition.

This unfortunate result was in great measure a result of the misconduct of the colonists themselves. Most of them were adventurers, who had embarked with no other expectation than that of getting together a fortune as speedily as possible in the golden Indies. They were without subordination, patience, industry, or any of the regular habits demanded for success in such an enterprise. As soon as they had launched from their native shore, they seemed to feel themselves released from the constraints of all law. They harbored jealousy and distrust of the admiral as a foreigner. The cavaliers and hidalgos (of whom there were too many in the expedition) condemned him as an upstart, whom it was derogatory to obey. From the first moment of their landing in Hispaniola, they indulged the most wanton license in regard to the unoffending natives, who, in the simplicity of their hearts, had received the white men as messengers from Heaven. Their outrages, however, soon provoked a general resistance, which led to a war of extermination. In less than four years after the Spaniards had set foot on the island, one-third of its population—amounting, probably, to several hundred thousands—were sacrificed! Such were the melancholy auspices, under which relations began between the civilized white man and the simple natives of the western world.

There was, in addition, a total neglect of agriculture, for none would condescend to turn up the earth for any other object than the gold they could find in it. This neglect, combined with the excesses practiced on the natives, at length occasioned an alarming scarcity of provisions. The poor Indians neglected their usual husbandry, being willing to starve themselves, so that they could starve out their oppressors. The Indians had some grounds for relying on the efficacy of starvation, if, as Las Casas gravely asserts, "one Spaniard consumed in a single day as much as would suffice three families!"

In order to avoid the famine which menaced his little colony, Columbus was obliged to resort to coercive measures, shortening the allowance of food, and compelling all to work, without distinction of rank. These unpalatable regulations soon bred general discontent. The high-mettled hidalgos, especially, complained loudly of the indignity of such drudgery, while Father Boil and his brethren were equally outraged by the diminution of their regular rations.

The Spanish sovereigns were now daily assailed with complaints of the mal-administration of Columbus, and of his severities to both Spaniards and natives. They lent, however, an unwilling ear to these vague accusations, for they fully appreciated the difficulties of his situation. Although they sent out an agent to inquire into the nature of the troubles which threatened the existence of the colony, they were careful to select an individual who they thought would be acceptable to the admiral. When Columbus in the following year (1496) returned to Spain, they received him with the most ample acknowledgments of regard. "Come to us," they said, in a kind letter of congratulation, "when you can do it without inconvenience to yourself, for you have endured too many vexations already."

The admiral brought with him, as before, such samples of the product of the western hemisphere, as would strike the public eye, and keep alive the feeling of curiosity. On his journey through Andalusia, he passed some

The signature of Christopher Columbus, a mystical
device in which the initials of Xristus, Maria, and
Yosephus (or Ysabel?) appear in the third line. The
name Christopher (*Christo-ferens*, literally Christ-
bearer) appears in the last line. The likeliest
interpretation is: *Servidor de Sus Altezas Sacras*
(Servant of Their Sacred Majesties) Christus,
Maria, Ysabel.

In later documents, Columbus' full titles are: *The
High Admiral of the Ocean, and Viceroy and Governor
General of the islands and mainland of Asia and the
Indies of the King and of the Queen, my Lords, and
their Captain General of the Sea, and Member of
their Council.*

days under the hospitable roof of the good curate, Bernaldez. A written memoir by this priest describes the remarkable appearance of the Indian chiefs following in the admiral's train, gorgeously decorated with golden collars and coronets and various barbaric ornaments. Among these he particularly notices certain "belts and masks of cotton and of wood, with figures of the Devil embroidered and carved thereon, sometimes in his own proper likeness, and at others in that of a cat or an owl. There is much reason," he infers, "to believe that he appears to the islanders in this guise, and that they are all idolaters, having Satan for their lord!"

But neither the attractions of the spectacle, nor the glowing representations of Columbus—who fancied he had discovered in the mines of Hispaniola the golden quarries of Ophir, from which King Solomon had enriched the temple of Jerusalem—could rekindle the dormant enthusiasm of the nation. The novelty of the thing had passed. They heard a different tale, moreover, from the other voyagers, whose wan and sallow visages provoked the bitter jest that they had returned with more gold in their faces than in their pockets. In short, the skepticism of the public seemed now quite in proportion to its former overweening confidence; and the returns were so meager, says Bernaldez, "that it was very generally believed there was little or no gold in the island."

Isabella was far from participating in this unreasonable distrust. She firmly relied on the admiral's repeated assurances, that the track of discovery would lead to other and more important regions. She formed a higher estimate, moreover, of the value of the new acquisitions than any founded on the actual proceeds in gold and silver. Her letters and instructions abundantly show that she kept ever in view the glorious purpose of introducing the blessings of Christian civilization among the heathen. She entertained a deep sense of the merits of Columbus, to whose serious and elevated character her own bore much resemblance.

But although the queen was willing to give the most effectual support to his great enterprise, the situation of the country made delay unavoidable. Large expense was necessarily incurred for the actual maintenance of the colony. The salaries alone, annually disbursed by the crown to persons resident in the colony, amounted to six million *maravédies*. The exchequer was liberally drained, moreover, by the Italian war, as well as by the magnificence with which the nuptials of the royal family were now celebrating. It was, indeed, in the midst of the courtly revelries attending the marriage of Prince John, that the admiral presented himself before the sovereigns at Burgos, after his second voyage. Such was the low condition of the treasury from these causes, that Isabella was obliged to defray the cost of an outfit to the colony, at this time, from funds originally destined for the marriage of her daughter Isabella with the king of Portugal.

This unwelcome delay, however, was softened to the

admiral by the distinguished marks which he daily received of the royal favor. Various ordinances were passed, confirming and enlarging his powers and privileges—to a greater extent, indeed, than his modesty, or his prudence, would allow him to accept. (Such, for example, was the grant of an immense tract of land in Hispaniola, with the title of count or duke, as the admiral might prefer.) The language in which these princely gratuities were conferred, rendered them doubly pleasing to his noble heart, containing, as they did, the most emphatic acknowledgments of his "many good, loyal, distinguished, and continual services."

Among the impediments to the immediate completion of the arrangements for the admiral's departure on his third voyage, there was also the hostility of Bishop Fonseca, who, at this period, had the control of the Indian department. He was a man of an irritable, and apparently unforgiving temper, who, from some displeasure arising previous to Columbus' second voyage, lost no opportunity of annoying and thwarting him.

Because of these various circumstances, the admiral's fleet was not ready before the beginning of 1498. Even then further embarrassment occurred in manning it, as few were found willing to embark in a service which had fallen into such general discredit. This led to the ruinous expedient of substituting convicts, whose regular punishments were commuted in exchange for a period of service in the Indies. No measure could possibly have been devised more effectual for the ruin of the infant settlement. The seeds of corruption, which had been so long festering in the Old World, soon shot up into a plentiful harvest in the New. Columbus, who suggested the measure, was the first to reap the fruits of it.

At length, all being in readiness, the admiral embarked on board his little squadron, consisting of six vessels. Their complement of men, notwithstanding every exertion, was still deficient when Columbus took his departure from the port of San Lúcar, May 30th, 1498. He steered in a more southerly direction than on his preceding voyages, and on the first of August succeeded in reaching *terra firma*, thus entitling himself to the glory of being the first to set foot on the great southern continent, to which he had before opened the way.

On his arrival at Hispaniola, Columbus found the affairs of the colony in confusion. An insurrection had been raised by a few factious individuals against his brother Bartholomew, to whom he had entrusted the government during his absence. In this desperate rebellion all the interests of the community were neglected. The mines, which were just beginning to yield a golden harvest, remained unworked. The unfortunate natives were subjected to the most inhuman oppression. There was no law but that of the strongest. Columbus, on his arrival, in vain endeavored to restore order. The very crews he brought with him, who had been unfortunately reprieved from the gibbet in their own country, served to swell the mass of mutiny.

The admiral exhausted art, negotiation, entreaty, force, and succeeded at length in patching up a specious reconciliation by concessions that essentially impaired his own authority. Among these was the grant of large tracts of land to the rebels, with permission to the proprietor to employ an allotted number of the natives in its cultivation. This was the origin of the celebrated system of *repartimientos*, which subsequently led to the foulest abuses that ever disgraced humanity.

In the meanwhile, rumors were every day reaching Spain of the distractions of the colony, accompanied with most injurious imputations on the conduct of Columbus and his brother. They were loudly accused of oppressing both Spaniards and Indians, and of sacrificing the public interests, in the most unscrupulous manner, to their own. These complaints were rung in the very ears of the sovereigns by numbers of the disaffected colonists, who had returned to Spain. These men surrounded the king as he rode out on horseback, clamoring loudly for the payment of the arrears, of which they said the admiral had defrauded them. Ferdinand Columbus mentions that he and his brother (who were then pages to the queen) could not stir out into the courtyard of the Alhambra, without being followed by fifty of these vagabonds, who insulted them in the grossest manner "as the sons of the adventurer, who had led so many brave Spanish hidalgos to seek their graves in the land of vanity and delusion."

Even some persons of high consideration at the court gave credence and circulation to these calumnies. The recent discovery of the pearl fisheries of Paria, as well as of more prolific veins of the precious metals in Hispaniola, and the prospect of an indefinite extent of unexplored country, opened by the late voyage of Columbus, made the viceroyalty of the New World a tempting bait for the avarice and ambition of the most potent grandees. They artfully endeavored, therefore, to undermine the admiral's standing with the sovereigns, by raising in their minds suspicions of his integrity. These they founded on letters received from the colony, charging him with disloyalty, with appropriating to his own use the revenues of the island, and with the design of erecting an independent government for himself.

Whatever weight these absurd charges may have had with Ferdinand, they had no power to shake the queen's confidence in Columbus, or lead her to suspect his loyalty for a moment. But the long-continued distractions of the colony made her feel a natural distrust of his capacity to govern it—whether from the jealousy entertained of him as a foreigner, or from some inherent deficiency in his own character. These doubts were strengthened by the arrival, at this juncture, of several of the rebels with the Indian slaves assigned to them by Columbus' orders.

It was the received opinion among good Catholics of that period, that heathen and barbarous nations were placed by the circumstance of their infidelity, beyond the reach of spiritual and civil rights. Their souls were doomed to eternal perdition. Their bodies were the property of any Christian nation who might occupy their soil. These were the maxims which regulated the Spanish and Portuguese navigators in their relations with the uncivilized natives of the western world. Columbus himself did not depart from these views. Very soon after the occupation of Hispaniola, he recommended a regular exchange of slaves for the commodities required for the support of the colony. He urged, moreover, that in this way their conversion would be more surely effected—an object, it must be admitted, which he seems at all times to have had most earnestly at heart.

Isabella, however, entertained views on this matter far more liberal than those of her age. She had been deeply interested by the accounts she had received from the admiral himself of the gentle, unoffending character of the islanders; and she revolted at the idea of consigning them to the horrors of slavery, without even an effort for their conversion. She hesitated, therefore, to sanction his proposal; and when a number of Indian captives were advertised to be sold in the markets of Andalusia, she commanded the sale to be suspended, till the counsel of theologians and doctors, learned in such matters, could be obtained. She urged that holy men be instructed as far as possible in the Indian languages, and sent out as missionaries for the conversion of the natives. Some of them (as

Father Boil and his brethren) seem, indeed, to have been more concerned for the welfare of their own bodies, than for the souls of their benighted flock. But others, imbued with a better spirit, wrought in the good work with disinterested zeal, and, if we may credit their accounts, with some efficacy.

In the same beneficent spirit, the royal letters and ordinances repeated over and over again the paramount obligation of the religious instruction of the natives, and of observing the utmost gentleness and humanity in all dealings with them. When, therefore, the queen learned of the arrival of two vessels from the Indies, with three hundred slaves on board, which the admiral had granted to the mutineers, she could not repress her indignation. "By what authority," she impatiently asked, "does Columbus venture thus to dispose of my subjects?" She instantly caused proclamation to be made in the southern provinces, that all who had Indian slaves in their possession, granted by the admiral, should forthwith provide for their return to their own country. The few still held by the crown were to be restored to freedom in like manner.

After a long and visible reluctance, the queen acquiesced in sending out a commissioner to investigate the affairs of the colony. The person appointed to this delicate trust was Don Francisco de Bobadilla, a poor knight of Calatrava. He was invested with supreme powers of civil and criminal jurisdiction. He was to bring to trial and pass sentence on all such as had conspired against the

authority of Columbus. He was authorized to take possession of the fortresses, vessels, public stores, and property
of every description, and to dispose of all offices. If he
deemed it expedient for the tranquility of the island, he
might command any persons, without distinction of rank,
to return to Spain, and present themselves before the
sovereigns. The original commission to Bobadilla was
dated March 21st, and May 21st, 1499; the execution of it,
however, was delayed until July, 1500—in the hope,
doubtless, that some news would come from Hispaniola
that would make the errand unnecessary.

It is impossible now to determine what motives could
have led to the selection of so incompetent an agent, for
an office of such high responsibility. He seems to have
been a weak and arrogant man, swelled up with the brief
authority thus undeservedly bestowed on him. From the
very first, he regarded Columbus as a convicted criminal,
on whom it was his business to execute the sentence of the
law. Accordingly, on his arrival at the island, after an
ostentatious parade of his credentials, he commanded the
admiral to appear before him. Without affecting the forms
of a legal inquiry, he caused him to be manacled, and
thrown into prison. Columbus submitted without the
least show of resistance, displaying in this sad reverse a
magnanimity of soul which would have touched the heart
of a generous adversary. Bobadilla, however, revealed no
such sensibility; after raking together all the foul or frivolous calumnies which hatred or the hope of favor could

extort, he caused the whole loathsome mass of accusation to be sent back to Spain with the admiral. Columbus himself he commanded to be kept strictly in irons during the passage, "afraid," wrote Ferdinand Columbus bitterly, "lest he might by any chance swim back again to the island."

This excess of malice served, however, to defeat itself. So enormous an outrage shocked the minds even of those most prejudiced against Columbus. All seemed to feel it as a national dishonor, that such indignities should be heaped on the man who, whatever might be his indiscretions, had done so much for Spain, and for the whole civilized world; a man, who, in the honest language of an old writer, "had he lived in the days of ancient Greece or Rome, would have had statues raised, and temples and divine honors dedicated to him, as to a divinity!" Ferdinand Columbus tells us that his father kept the fetters in which he was brought home, hanging up in an apartment of his house, as a perpetual memorial of national ingratitude, and, when he died, ordered them to be buried in the same grave with himself.

None partook of the general indignation more strongly than Ferdinand and Isabella. In addition to their personal feelings of disgust at so gross an act, they clearly understood that it reflected badly on themselves. They sent to Cadiz without an instant's delay, and commanded the admiral to be released from his fetters. They wrote to him expressing their sincere regret for the unworthy usage which he had experienced, and requesting him to appear before them as speedily as possible at Granada, where the court was then staying. At the same time, they furnished him a thousand ducats for his expenses, and a handsome retinue to escort him on his journey.

Columbus, revived by these assurances of the kind dispositions of his sovereigns, proceeded without delay to Granada, which he reached on the 17th of December. Immediately on his arrival he obtained an audience. The queen could not repress her tears at the sight of the man, whose undeserved misfortunes were chargeable, in part, to herself. She endeavored to cheer his wounded spirit with the most earnest assurances of her sympathy and sorrow for his misfortunes. Columbus, from the first moment of his disgrace, had relied on the good faith and kindness of Isabella; for, as an ancient Castilian writer remarks, "she had ever favored him beyond the king her husband, protecting his interests, and showing him especial kindness and good-will." When he beheld the emotion of his royal mistress, and listened to her consolatory language, it was too much for his loyal and generous heart; throwing himself on his knees, he gave vent to his feelings, and sobbed aloud. The sovereigns endeavored to soothe and tranquilize his mind, and promised him that impartial justice should be done his enemies, and that he should be reinstated in his benefits and honors.

Although the king and queen determined without hesitation on the complete restoration of the admiral's honors, they thought it better to defer his reappointment to the government of the colony, until the present disturbances should be settled, and he might return there with personal safety and advantage. In the meantime, they resolved to send out a competent individual, and to support him with such a force as should overawe faction, and enable him to place the tranquility of the island on a permanent basis.

The person selected was Don Nicolas de Ovando, *comendador* of Lares, of the military order of Alcántara. This was a man of acknowledged prudence and sagacity, temperate in his habits, and plausible and politic in his address. It is sufficient evidence of his standing at court, that he had been one of the ten youths selected to be educated in the palace as companions for the prince of the Asturias. He was furnished with a fleet of two and thirty sail, carrying twenty-five hundred persons, many of them of the best families in the kingdom, with every variety of article for the nourishment and permanent prosperity of the colony. The general equipment was in a style of expense and magnificence, such as had never before been lavished on any armada destined for the western waters.

The new governor was instructed immediately on his arrival to send Bobadilla home for trial. Under his lax administration, abuses of every kind had multiplied to an alarming extent, and the poor natives were rapidly wasting away under the new and most inhuman arrangement of the *repartimientos*, which he established. Isabella now declared the Indians free; she emphatically required the authorities of Hispaniola to respect them as true and faithful vassals of the crown. Ovando was especially to ascertain the amount of losses sustained by Columbus and his brothers, and to provide for their full indemnification.

Fortified with the most ample instructions in regard to these and other details of his administration, the governor embarked on board his magnificent flotilla, and crossed the bar of San Lúcar, February 15th, 1502. A furious tempest dispersed the fleet, before it had been out a week, and a report reached Spain that it had entirely perished. The sovereigns, overwhelmed with sorrow at this fresh disaster, which consigned so many of their best and bravest to a watery grave, shut themselves up in their palace for several days. Fortunately, the report proved ill-founded. The fleet rode out the storm in safety, one vessel only having perished; the remainder reached in due time its place of destination.

- 4 -

The House of Trade

Ferdinand and Isabella manifested from the first an eager and enlightened curiosity in reference to their new acquisitions. They interrogated the admiral constantly and minutely as to the soil and climate of the Indies, their various vegetable and mineral products, and especially the character of the uncivilized races who inhabited them. They paid the greatest deference to his suggestions, as before remarked, and liberally supplied the infant settlement with whatever could contribute to its nourishment and permanent prosperity. Through their provident attention, in a very few years after its discovery, the island of Hispaniola was in possession of the most important domestic animals, as well as fruits and vegetables of the Old World, some of which have since continued to furnish the staple of a far more lucrative commerce than was ever anticipated from its gold mines.

Emigration to the new countries was encouraged by royal ordinances. The settlers in Hispaniola were to have their passage free; to be excused from taxes; to have the absolute property of such plantations on the island as they should engage to cultivate for four years; and they were furnished with a supply of grain and stock for their farms. All exports and imports were exempted from duty, a striking contrast to the narrow policy of later ages. Five hundred persons, including scientific men and artisans of every description, were sent out and maintained at the expense of government. To provide for the greater security and quiet of the island, Governor Ovando was authorized to gather the residents into towns, which were endowed with all the privileges of similar corporations in the mother country; and a number of married men, with their families, were encouraged to establish themselves in them, with the view of giving greater solidity and permanence to the settlement.

With these wise provisions were mingled others savoring too strongly of the illiberal spirit of the age. Such were those prohibiting Jews, Moors, or indeed any but Castilians—for whom the discovery was considered exclusively to have been made—from inhabiting, or even visiting, the New World. The exclusion of foreigners, at least all but "Catholic Christians," is particularly recommended by Columbus in his first communication to the crown. The government reserved to itself the exclusive possession of all minerals, dyewoods, and precious stones, that should be discovered; and although private persons were allowed to search for gold, they were subjected to the exorbitant tax of two-thirds (subsequently reduced to one-fifth) of all they should obtain, for the crown.

One measure contributed more effectually than any other, at this period, to the progress of discovery and colonization. This was the license granted, under certain regulations, in 1495, for voyages undertaken by private individuals. No use was made of this permission until some years later, in 1499. The spirit of enterprise had flagged, and the nation had experienced something like disappointment on contrasting the meager results of their own discoveries with the dazzling successes of the Portuguese, who had struck at once into the very heart of the jewelled east. The report of the admiral's third voyage, however, and the beautiful specimens of pearls which he sent home from the coast of Paria, revived the cupidity of the nation. Foreign adventurers, meanwhile, had begun to follow in the track of Columbus.* The Spanish government willingly acquiesced in a measure, which, while it opened a wide field of enterprise for its subjects, secured to itself all the substantial benefits of discovery, without any of the burdens.

The ships fitted out under the general license were

* Among these were the two Cabots, who sailed in the service of the English monarch, Henry VII, in 1497, and ran down the whole coast of North America, from Newfoundland to within a few degrees of Florida, thus encroaching, as it were, on the very field of discovery preoccupied by the Spaniards.

required to reserve one-tenth of their tonnage for the crown, as well as two-thirds of all the gold, and ten per cent of all other commodities which they should procure. The government promoted these expeditions by a bounty on all vessels of six hundred tons and upwards, engaged in them.

With this encouragement the more wealthy merchants of Seville, Cádiz, and Palos freighted and sent out little squadrons of three or four vessels each, which they entrusted to the experienced mariners who had accompanied Columbus in his first voyage, or since followed in his footsteps. They held in general the same course pursued by the admiral on his last expedition, exploring the coasts of the great southern continent. Some of the adventurers returned with rich freights of gold, pearls, and other precious commodities, that well compensated the fatigues and perils of the voyage. But the greater number were obliged to content themselves with the more enduring but barren honors of discovery.

The active spirit of enterprise that was now awakened, and the more enlarged commercial relations with the new colonies, required a more perfect organization of the department for Indian affairs. By an ordinance dated at Alcalá, January 20th, 1503, it was provided that a board should be established, consisting of three functionaries, with the titles of treasurer, factor, and comptroller. Their permanent residence was assigned in the old *alcázar* of Seville, where they were to meet every day for the despatch of business. The board was expected to make itself thoroughly acquainted with whatever concerned the colonies, and to afford the government all information, that could be obtained, affecting their interests and commercial prosperity. It was empowered to grant licenses under the regular conditions, to provide for the equipment of fleets, to determine their destination, and furnish them instructions on sailing. All merchandise for exportation was to be deposited in the alcázar, where the return cargoes were to be received, and contracts made for their sale. Similar authority was given to it over the trade with the Barbary coast and the Canary Islands. Its supervision was to extend in like manner over all vessels which might take their departure from the port of Cádiz, as well as from Seville. With these powers were combined others of a purely judicial character, authorizing them to take cognizance of questions arising out of particular voyages, and of the colonial trade in general. In this latter capacity they were to be assisted by the advice of two jurists, maintained by a regular salary from the government.

Such were the extensive powers entrusted to the famous *Casa de Contratación*, or House of Trade, on this its first definite organization. Although its authority was subsequently somewhat limited by the appellate jurisdiction of the Council of the Indies, it always continued to be the great organ by which the commercial transactions with the colonies were conducted and controlled.

The Spanish government thus secured to itself the

more easy and exclusive management of the colonial trade, by confining it within one narrow channel. At the same time, it arranged for its absolute supremacy in ecclesiastical affairs, where alone it could be contested. By a bull of Alexander the Sixth, dated November 16th, 1501, the sovereigns were empowered to receive all the tithes in the colonial dominions. Another bull, of Pope Julius the Second, July 28th, 1508, granted them the right of appointing to all benefices, of whatever description, in the colonies, subject only to the approbation of the Holy See. By these two concessions, the Spanish crown was placed at once at the head of the church in its transatlantic dominions, with the absolute disposal of all its dignities and emoluments.

More than one historian has found it remarkable that Ferdinand and Isabella, with their reverence for the Catholic church, should have had the courage to assume an attitude of such entire independence of its spiritual chief. But whoever has studied their reign, will regard this measure as perfectly in keeping with their habitual policy, which never allowed a blind deference to the church to compromise in any degree the independence of the crown. It is much more astonishing, that pontiffs could be found content to part with such important prerogatives. It was deviating widely from the subtle and tenacious spirit of their predecessors; and, as the consequences came to be more fully disclosed, furnished ample subject of regret to those who succeeded them.

Such is a brief summary of the principal regulations adopted by Ferdinand and Isabella for the administration of the colonies. Many of their peculiarities, including most of their defects, are to be referred to the peculiar circumstances under which the discovery of the New World was effected. Unlike the settlements on the comparatively sterile shores of North America (which were permitted to devise laws accommodated to their necessities, and to gather strength in the habitual exercise of political functions), the Spanish colonies were from the very first checked and controlled by the over-legislation of the parent country. The original project of discovery had been entered into with indefinite expectations of gain. The verification of Columbus' theory of the existence of land in the west made it easier to believe his other conjecture: that that land was the far-famed Indies. The specimens of gold and other precious commodities found there, served to maintain the delusion. The Spanish government regarded the expedition as its own private adventure, to whose benefits it had exclusive pretensions. Hence those jealous regulations for securing to itself a monopoly of the most obvious sources of profit, the dyewoods and precious metals.

These impolitic provisions were relieved by others better suited to the permanent interests of the colony. Such were the various bounties offered on the occupation and culture of land, the erection of municipalities, the right of inter-colonial traffic, and of exporting and importing merchandise of every description free of duty. These and similar laws show that the government did not regard the colonies merely as a foreign acquisition to be sacrificed to the interests of the mother country (as later occurred), but was disposed to legislate for them on more generous principles, as an integral portion of the monarchy.

It would not be giving a fair view of the great objects proposed by the Spanish sovereigns in their schemes of discovery, to omit one which was paramount to all the rest, with the queen at least—the propagation of Christianity among the heathen. The conversion and civilization of this simple people form, as has been already said, the burden of most of her official communications from the earliest period. She neglected no means for the furtherance of this good work, through the agency of missionaries exclusively devoted to it, who were to establish their residence among the natives, and win them to the true faith by their instructions, and the edifying example of their own lives. It was with the intent of improving the condition of the natives, that she sanctioned the introduction into the colonies of negro slaves born in Spain. This she did in the belief that the physical constitution of the African was much better fitted than that of the Indian to endure severe toil under a tropical climate. To this false principle of economizing human suffering, we are indebted for that foul stain on the New World, which grew deeper and darker with the lapse of years.

Isabella, however, was destined to have her benevolent designs, in regard to the natives, defeated by her own subjects. The popular doctrine of the absolute rights of the Christian over the heathen became a license for the exaction of labor from these unhappy beings, to any degree which avarice on the one hand could demand, or human endurance concede on the other. The device of the repartimientos systematized and completed the whole scheme of oppression. The queen, it is true, abolished them under Ovando's administration, and declared the Indians "as free as her own subjects." It was claimed, however, that the Indians, when no longer compelled to work, withdrew from all intercourse with the Christians, thus annihilating at once all hopes of their conversion. This argument induced the queen to consent that they should be required to labor moderately and for a reasonable compensation. The colonists interpreted this consent in the broadest manner possible. They soon revived the old system on so terrific a scale, that a letter of Columbus, written shortly after Isabella's death, claims more than six-sevenths of the whole population of Hispaniola to have melted away under it!

The queen was too far removed to enforce the execution of her own beneficent measures; nor is it probable, that she ever imagined the extent of their violation, for there was no intrepid philanthropist, in that day, like Las Casas, to proclaim to the world the wrongs and sorrows of the Indian.* A conviction, however, of the unworthy treatment of the natives seems to have pressed heavily on her heart; in a codicil to her testament, dated a few days before her death, she invokes the kind offices of her successor in their behalf, in strong and affectionate language that plainly indicates how intently her thoughts were occupied with their condition down to the last hour of her existence.

The moral grandeur of the maritime discoveries under this reign must not so far dazzle us, as to lead to a very high estimate of their immediate results in an economical view. Most of those articles which have since formed the great staples of South American commerce—as cocoa, indigo, cochineal, tobacco, etc.—were either not known in Isabella's time, or not cultivated for exportation. Small quantities of cotton had been brought to Spain, but it was doubted whether the profit would compensate the expense of raising it. The sugar cane had been transplanted into Hispaniola, and thrived luxuriantly. But it required time to grow it to any considerable amount as an article of commerce; and this was still further delayed by the distractions as well as the avarice of the colony, which grasped at nothing less substantial than gold itself. The only vegetable produce extensively used in trade was the brazil-wood, whose beautiful dye and application to various ornamental purposes made it, from the first, one of

---

* Bartolomé De Las Casas made his first voyage to the Indies in 1498, or at latest 1502; but there is no trace of his taking an active part in denouncing the oppressions of the Spaniards earlier than 1510, when he combined his efforts with those of the Dominican missionaries lately arrived in St. Domingo, in the same good work. It was not until some years later, 1515, that he returned to Spain and pleaded the cause of the injured natives before the throne.

the most important monopolies of the crown.

The accounts are too vague to provide any probable estimate of the precious metals obtained from the new territories previous to Ovando's mission. Before the discovery of the mines of Hayna it was certainly not very great. The size of some of the specimens of ore found there suggested magnificent ideas of their opulence. One piece of gold is reported by the contemporary historians to have weighed three thousand two hundred castellanos, and to have been so large, that the Spaniards served up a roasted pig on it, boasting that no potentate in Europe could dine off so costly a dish. The admiral's own statement, that the miners obtained from six gold castellanos to one hundred or even two hundred and fifty in a day, allows a latitude too great to lead to any definite conclusion. To this testimony might be added that of the well-informed historian of Seville, who infers from several royal ordinances that the influx of the precious metals had been such, before the close of the fifteenth century, as to affect the value of the currency and the regular prices of commodities.

These large estimates, however, are scarcely reconcilable with the popular discontent at the meagerness of the returns obtained from the New World, or with the assertion of Bernaldez (of the same date with Zuñiga's reference) that "so little gold had been brought home as to raise a general belief that there was scarcely any in the island." There are frequent assertions by contemporary writers, that the expenses of the colonies considerably exceeded the profits. This may account for the very limited scale on which the Spanish government pursued its schemes of discovery, as compared with its Portuguese neighbors, who followed up theirs with a magnificent apparatus of fleets and armies, that could have been supported only by the teeming treasures of the eastern Indies.

Whatever be the amount of physical good or evil immediately resulting to Spain from her new discoveries, their moral consequences were inestimable. The ancient limits of human thought and action were overleaped; the veil which had covered the secrets of the deep for so many centuries was removed; another hemisphere was thrown open; and a boundless expansion promised to science, from the infinite varieties in which nature was exhibited in these unexplored regions. The success of the Spaniards kindled a generous emulation in their Portuguese rivals, who soon after accomplished their long-sought passage into the Indian seas, and thus completed the great circle of maritime discovery.

It would seem as if Providence had postponed this grand event until the possession of America, with its stores of precious metals, might supply such materials for a commerce with the east, as should bind together the most distant quarters of the globe. The impression made on the enlightened minds of that day is evinced by their tone of gratitude and exultation at being permitted to witness these glorious events, which their fathers had so long, but in vain, desired to see.

-5-

The Last Voyage

The Spanish government has been strenuously criticized for its injustice and ingratitude in delaying to restore Columbus to the full possession of his colonial authority. But this appears to be wholly undeserved. It was obviously inadvisable to return him immediately to Hispaniola before the embers of animosity there had had time to cool. In addition, there were several features in his character, which make it doubtful whether he was the most competent person, in any event, for an emergency demanding the greatest coolness, combined with acknowledged personal authority. His sublime enthusiasm, which carried him victorious over every obstacle, involved him also in numerous embarrassments, which men of duller temperament would have escaped. It led him to count too readily on a similar spirit in others—

and to be disappointed. It gave an exaggerated coloring to his views and descriptions, that inevitably led to a reaction in the minds of those who ventured all on the splendid dreams of a fairy land, which they were never to realize.* It led him, in his eagerness for the achievement of his great enterprises, to be less scrupulous and politic as to the means, than a less ardent spirit would have been. His tenacious adherence to the scheme of Indian slavery, and his impolitic regulation compelling the labor of the hidalgos, are examples of this. He was, moreover, a foreigner, without rank, fortune, or powerful friends; and his high and sudden elevation naturally raised him up a thousand enemies among a proud, punctilious, and intensely national people. The sovereigns might well be excused for not entrusting Columbus, at this delicate crisis, with disentangling the meshes of intrigue and faction in which the affairs of the colony were so unhappily involved.

It is more difficult to excuse the paltry equipment with which the admiral was provided on the occasion of his fourth and last voyage. The object proposed by this expedition was the discovery of a passage to the great Indian Ocean. This, he inferred (sagaciously enough from his premises, but in fact, most erroneously) must open some-

* The high devotional feeling of Columbus led him to trace out allusions in Scripture to the various circumstances and scenes of his adventurous life. Thus he believed his great discovery announced in the Apocalypse, and in Isaiah; he identified, as I have before stated, the mines of Hispaniola with those which furnished Solomon with materials for his temple; he fancied that he had determined the actual locality of the garden of Eden in the newly discovered region of Paria.

where between Cuba and the coast of Paria. Four cara-vels, only, were furnished for the expedition, the largest of which did not exceed seventy tons' burden. This was in striking contrast to the magnificent armada lately en-trusted to Ovando. [See pages 65-66, Editor]

Columbus, oppressed with growing infirmities, and a consciousness, perhaps, of the decline of popular favor, showed an unusual despondency as he waited to embark. He talked even of resigning the task of further discovery to his brother Bartholomew. "I have established," said he, "all that I proposed—the existence of land in the west. I have opened the gate, and others may enter at their pleasure; as indeed they do, arrogating to themselves the title of discoverers, to which they can have little claim, following as they do in my track." He little thought the ingratitude of mankind would sanction the claims of these adventurers so far as to confer the name of one of them—Amerigo Vespucci—on that world which his genius had revealed.

The great inclination, however, which the admiral had to serve the Catholic sovereigns, induced him to lay aside his scruples, and encounter the perils and fatigues of another voyage. A few weeks before his departure, he received a gracious letter from Ferdinand and Isabella, the last ever addressed to him by his royal mistress, assuring him of their purpose to maintain inviolate all their engagements with him, and to perpetuate the inheritance of his honors in his family.* Comforted and cheered by these assurances, the veteran navigator, quitting the port of Cádiz on the 9th of March, 1502, once more spread his sails for those golden regions, which he had approached so near, but was destined never to reach.

The admiral had received instructions not to touch at Hispaniola on his outward voyage. The leaky condition of one of his ships, however, and the signs of an approaching storm, induced him to seek a temporary refuge there. At the same time, he counselled Ovando to delay for a few days the departure of the fleet, then riding in the harbor, which was destined to carry Bobadilla and the rebels with their ill-gotten treasures back to Spain. The churlish governor, however, not only refused Columbus admittance, but gave orders for the instant departure of the vessels.

The apprehensions of the experienced mariner were fully justified by the event. Scarcely had the Spanish fleet quitted its moorings, before one of those tremendous hurricanes came on, which so often desolate these tropical regions, sweeping down everything before it. It fell with such violence on the little navy, that out of eighteen ships, only three or four escaped. The rest all foundered, including those which contained Bobadilla and the late enemies of Columbus. Two hundred thousand *castellanos* of gold, half of which belonged to the government, went to the bottom with them. The only one of the fleet which

* Among other instances of the queen's personal regard for Columbus, may be noticed her receiving his two sons, Diego and Fernando, as her own pages, on the death of Prince John, in whose service they had formerly been.

made its way back to Spain was a cracked and weather-beaten bark which contained the admiral's property, amounting to four thousand ounces of gold. To complete these curious coincidences, Columbus with his little squadron rode out the storm in safety under the lee of the island, where he had prudently taken shelter on being so rudely repulsed from the port. This combination of events led many to discern the hand of Providence. Others, in a less Christian temper, referred it all to the necromancy of the admiral.

Columbus' fourth and last voyage was one unbroken series of disappointment and disaster. After quitting Hispaniola, and being driven by storms nearly to the island of Cuba, he traversed the Gulf of Honduras, and coasted along the margin of the golden region, which had so long flitted before his fancy. In vain, the natives invited him to strike into its western depths and he pressed forward to the south, now solely occupied with the grand object of discovering a passage into the Indian Ocean. At length, after having with great difficulty advanced somewhat beyond the point of Nombre de Dios, he was compelled by the fury of the elements, and the murmurs of his men, to abandon the enterprise, and retrace his steps. He was subsequently defeated in an attempt to establish a colony on terra firma, by the ferocity of the natives. Wrecked on the island of Jamaica, he was permitted to linger more than a year, through the malice of Ovando, the new governor of Santo Domingo. Finally, having reembarked with his shattered crew in a vessel freighted at his own expense, he was driven by a succession of terrible tempests across the ocean, until, on the 7th of November, 1504, he anchored in the little port of San Lúcar, twelve leagues from Seville.

In this quiet haven, Columbus hoped to find the repose his broken constitution and wounded spirit so much needed, and to obtain a speedy restitution of his honors and emoluments from the hand of Isabella. But here he was to experience his bitterest disappointment. At the time of his arrival, the queen was on her deathbed; and in a very few days Columbus received the afflicting news that the friend, on whose steady support he had so long relied, was no more. It was a heavy blow to his hopes, for "he had always experienced favor and protection from her," says his son Ferdinand, "while the king had not only been indifferent, but positively unfriendly to his interests." We may readily believe that a man of the cold and prudent character of the Aragonese monarch would not be very likely to comprehend one so ardent and aspiring as that of Columbus. And, if nothing has hitherto met our eye to warrant the strong language of the son, yet we have seen that the king, from the first, distrusted the admiral's projects, as having something unsound and chimerical in them.

The affliction of Columbus at the tidings of Isabella's death is strongly depicted in a letter written immediately after to his son Diego. "It is our chief duty," he says, "to commend to God most affectionately and devoutly the soul of our deceased lady, the queen. Her life was always Catholic and virtuous, and prompt to whatever could redound to His holy service; wherefore, we may trust, she now rests in glory, far from all concern for this rough and weary world."

Columbus, at this time, was so much crippled by the gout, to which he had been long subject, that he was unable to undertake a journey to Segovia, where the court was, during the winter. He hastened, however, to lay his situation before the king through his son Diego, who was attached to the royal household. He recounted his past services, the original terms of the capitulation made with him, their infringement in almost every particular, and his own needy condition. But Ferdinand was too occupied with his own concerns, at this crisis, to give much heed to those of Columbus. At length, on the approach of a milder season, the admiral was able by easy journeys to reach Segovia, and present himself before the monarch. He was received with all the outward marks of courtesy and regard by Ferdinand, who assured him that "he fully estimated his important services, and, far from stinting his recompense to the precise terms of the capitulation, intended to confer more ample favors on him in Castile."

These fair words, however, were not seconded by actions. The king probably had no serious thoughts of reinstating the admiral in his government. His successor,

Ovando, was high in the royal favor. His rule, however objectionable as regards the Indians, was every way acceptable to the Spanish colonists; and his oppression of the poor natives enabled him to pour much larger sums into the royal coffers than had been gleaned by his more humane predecessor.

The events of the last voyage, moreover, had not tended to dispel any distrust which the king may have felt of the admiral's capacity for government. His men had been in a state of perpetual insubordination; while his letter to the sovereigns, written from Jamaica, under distressing circumstances, exhibited such a deep coloring of despondency, and occasionally such wild and visionary projects, as might almost suggest a temporary alienation of mind. This document exhibits a medley, in which sober narrative and sound reasoning are strangely blended with crazy dreams, doleful lamentation, and wild schemes for the recovery of Jerusalem, the conversion of the Grand Khan, etc. Vagaries like these, which come occasionally like clouds over his soul, to shut out the light of reason, cannot fail to fill the mind of the reader, as they doubtless did those of the sovereigns at the time, with mingled sentiments of wonder and compassion.

But whatever reasons may have operated to postpone Columbus' restoration to power, it was the grossest injustice to withhold from him the revenues secured by the original contract with the crown. According to his own statement, he was so far from receiving his share of the remittances made by Ovando, that he was obliged to borrow money, and had actually incurred a heavy debt for his necessary expenses. The truth was that, as the resources of the new countries began to develop themselves more abundantly, Ferdinand felt greater reluctance to comply with the letter of the original capitulation; he now considered the compensation as too vast and altogether disproportioned to the services of any subject. At length he was so ungenerous as to propose that the admiral should relinquish his claims, in consideration of other estates and dignities to be assigned him in Castile. It manifested less knowledge of character than the king usually showed, that he should have thought the man, who had broken off all negotiations on the threshold of a dubious enterprise, rather than abate one tittle of his demands, would consent to such abatement when the success of that enterprise was so gloriously established.

What assistance Columbus actually received from the crown at this time, or whether he received any, does not appear. He continued to reside with the court, and accompanied it in its removal to Valladolid. He no doubt enjoyed the public consideration due to his high repute and extraordinary achievements; though by the monarch he might be regarded in the unwelcome light of a creditor, whose claims were too just to be disavowed, and too large to be satisfied.

With spirits broken by this unthankful requital of his services, and with a constitution impaired by a life of unmitigated hardship, Columbus' health now rapidly sank under the severe and reiterated attacks of his disorder. On the arrival of Philip and Joanna, he addressed a letter to them, through his brother Bartholomew, in which he lamented the infirmities which prevented him from paying his respects in person, and made an offer of his future services. The communication was graciously received, but Columbus did not survive to behold the young sovereigns.*

His mental vigor, however, was not impaired by the ravages of disease, and on the 19th day of May, 1506, he executed a codicil, confirming certain dispositions formerly made, with special reference to the entail of his estates and dignities. This latest act manifested the same solicitude he had shown through life, to perpetuate an honorable name. Having completed these arrangements with perfect composure, he expired on the following day, being then something near seventy years of age, with little apparent suffering, and in the most Christian spirit of resignation. His remains, first deposited in the convent of St. Francis at Valladolid, were, six years later, removed to the Carthusian monastery of Las Cuevas at Seville, where a costly monument was raised over them by King Ferdinand, with the memorable inscription,

"A Castilla y á Leon
Nuevo mundo dió Colon"

* Joanna, the third child of Isabella and Ferdinand, married Philip of Burgundy. [Editor]

To Castile and to Leon
Columbus gave a new world.

"the like of which," says his son Ferdinand, with as much truth as simplicity, "was never recorded of any man in ancient or modern times." From this spot his body was transported, in the year 1536, to the island of Santo Domingo, the proper theater of his discoveries; and, on the cession of the island to the French, in 1795, was again removed to Cuba, where his ashes now quietly repose in the cathedral church of its capital, Havana.

While the colonial empire of Spain was thus every day enlarging, the man to whom it was all due was never permitted to know the extent or the value of it. He died in the conviction in which he lived, that the land he had reached was the long-sought Indies. But it was a country far richer than the Indies; and, had he on quitting Cuba struck into a westerly, instead of southerly direction, it would have carried him into the very depths of the golden regions, whose existence he had so long and vainly predicted. As it was, he "only opened the gates," to use his own language, for others more fortunate than himself. Before he quitted Hispaniola for the last time, the young adventurer arrived there, who was destined, by the conquest of Mexico, to realize all the magnificent visions, which had been derided as only visions, in the lifetime of Columbus.*

* Prescott here refers to Hernán Cortés, who inspired the historian's most famous work, *History of the Conquest of Mexico* (1843).

-6-

Character of the Sovereigns, and of Their Policies

I t is in the undying attachment of the Spanish nation that we see the strongest testimony to the virtues of Isabella. We shall see but one judgment formed of her, whether by foreigners or natives. The French and Italian writers equally join in celebrating the triumphant glories of her reign, and her magnanimity, wisdom, and purity of character. Her own subjects extol her as "the most brilliant exemplar of every virtue," and mourn over the day of her death as "the last of the prosperity and happiness of their country."

Her person was of middle height, and well proportioned. She had a clear, fresh complexion, with light blue eyes and auburn hair—a style of beauty exceedingly rare in Spain. The portraits that remain of her combine a faultless symmetry of features with singular sweetness and intelligence of expression.

Her manners were marked by natural dignity and modest reserve, tempered by an affability which flowed from the kindliness of her disposition. She showed great tact in accommodating herself to the peculiar situation and character of those around her. She appeared in arms at the head of her troops, and shrunk from none of the hardships of war. During the reforms introduced into the religious houses, she visited the nunneries in person, taking her needle-work with her, and passing the day in the society of the inmates. When travelling in Galicia, she attired herself in the costume of the country, borrowing for that purpose the jewels and other ornaments of the ladies there, and returning them with liberal additions.

She spoke the Castilian with elegance and correctness and had an easy fluency of discourse, occasionally seasoned with wit. She was temperate in her diet, seldom or never tasting wine, and so frugal in her table, that the daily expenses for herself and family did not exceed the moderate sum of forty ducats. She was equally simple and economical in her apparel. On all public occasions, indeed, she displayed a royal magnificence; but she had no relish for it in private, and she freely gave away her clothes and jewels, as presents to her friends. Naturally of a sedate, though cheerful temper, she had little taste for the frivolous amusements which make up so much of a court life; and, if she encouraged the presence of minstrels and musicians in her palace, it was to wean her young nobility from the coarser pleasures to which they were addicted.

During the first busy and bustling years of her reign, she was almost always in the saddle, for she made all her journeys on horseback; and she travelled with a rapidity, which made her always present on the spot where her presence was needed. She was never intimidated by the weather, or the state of her own health; and this reckless exposure undoubtedly contributed much to impair her excellent constitution.

She was equally indefatigable in her mental application. After careful attention to business through the day, she was often known to sit up all night, dictating despatches to her secretaries. In the midst of these overwhelming cares, she found time to supply the defects of her early education by learning Latin, so as to understand it without difficulty, whether written or spoken. As she had little turn for light amusements, she sought relief from graver cares by some useful occupation appropriate to her sex; and she left ample evidence of her skill in this way, in the rich specimens of embroidery, wrought with her own fair hands, with which she decorated the churches. She was careful to instruct her daughters in these more humble departments of domestic duty; for she thought nothing too humble to learn, which was useful.

Her schemes were vast, and executed in the same noble spirit in which they were conceived. She never employed doubtful agents or sinister measures, but the most direct and open policy. Where she had once given her confidence, she gave her hearty and steady support.

Isabella's measures were characterized by practical good sense. Though engaged all her life in reforms, she had none of the failings so common in reformers. Her plans, though vast, were never visionary. The best proof of this is, that she lived to see most of them realized.

But the principle, which gave a peculiar coloring to every feature of Isabella's mind, was piety. It shone forth from the very depths of her soul with a heavenly radiance, which illuminated her whole character. Her earliest years had been passed in the rugged school of adversity, under the eye of a mother who implanted in her serious mind such strong principles of religion as nothing in after life could shake.

Her piety was strikingly exhibited in that unfeigned humility, which, although the very essence of our faith, is so rarely found—and most rarely in those whose great powers and exalted stations seem to raise them above the level of ordinary mortals. Unfortunately, that humility which made her defer so reverentially to her ecclesiastical advisers, led, under the fanatic Torquemada, to those deep blemishes on her administration, the establishment of the Inquisition and the exile of the Jews.

But, though these are blemishes of the deepest dye on her administration, they can not be regarded as such on her moral character. It will be difficult to condemn her, indeed, without condemning the age; for these very acts are not only excused, but extolled by her contemporaries, as constituting her strongest claims to renown, and to the gratitude of her country.

Whatever errors of judgment may be imputed to her, she most anxiously sought in all situations to discern and discharge her duty. Faithful in the dispensation of justice, no bribe was large enough to ward off the execution of the law. No motive, not even conjugal affection, could induce her to make an unsuitable appointment to public office. No reverence for the ministers of religion could lead her to wink at their misconduct, nor could the deference she entertained for the head of the church, allow her to tolerate his encroachments on the rights of her crown.

She seemed to consider herself especially bound to preserve entire the peculiar claims and privileges of Castile, after its union under the same sovereign with Aragon. While her own will was law, she governed in such a manner that it might appear the joint action of both Ferdinand and herself. Yet she was careful never to surrender into his hands any of those prerogatives which belonged to her as queen proprietor of the kingdom.

"King Ferdinand was of the middle size," says a contemporary, who knew him well. "His complexion was fresh; his eyes bright and animated; his nose and mouth small and finely formed, and his teeth white; his forehead lofty and serene; with flowing hair of a bright chestnut color. His manners were courteous, and his countenance seldom clouded by anything like spleen or melancholy. He was grave in speech and action, and had a marvellous dignity of presence. His whole demeanor, in fine, was truly that of a great king." For this flattering portrait Ferdinand must have sat at an earlier and happier period of his life.

His education, owing to the troubled state of the times, had been neglected in his boyhood, though he was early instructed in all the generous pastimes and exercises of chivalry. He was esteemed one of the most perfect horsemen of his court. He led an active life, and the only kind of reading he appeared to relish was history. The only amusement for which he cared much was hunting, especially falconry, and that he never carried to excess till his last years. He was indefatigable in application to business. He had no relish for the pleasures of the table, and, like Isabella, was temperate even to abstemiousness in his diet.

He was frugal in his domestic and personal expenditure, partly, no doubt, from a willingness to rebuke the opposite spirit of wastefulness and ostentation in his nobles. He lost no good opportunity of doing this. On one occasion, it is said, he turned to a gallant of the court noted for his extravagance in dress, and laying his hand on his own doublet, exclaimed, "Excellent stuff this; it has lasted me three pair of sleeves!"

His income was moderate, his enterprises numerous and vast. It was impossible that he could meet them without husbanding his resources with the most careful economy. No one has accused him of attempting to enrich his exchequer by the venal sale of office, like Louis the Twelfth, or by griping extortion, like another royal contemporary, Henry the Seventh. He amassed no treasure, and indeed died so poor, that he left scarcely enough in his coffers to defray the charges of his funeral.

Ferdinand was devout; at least he was scrupulous in regard to the exterior of religion. He was punctual in attendance on mass; careful to observe all the ordinances and ceremonies of his church; and left many tokens of his piety, after the fashion of the time, in sumptuous edifices and endowments for religious purposes. His Catholic zeal was observed to be marvelously efficacious in furthering his temporal interests. His most objectionable enterprises, even, were covered with a veil of religion. In this, however, he did not much differ from the practice of the age. Some of the most scandalous wars of that period were ostensibly at the bidding of the church, or in defense of Christendom against the infidel. This display of a religious motive was very usual with the Spanish and Portuguese. The crusading spirit, nourished by their struggle with the Moors and subsequently by their African and American expeditions, gave a habitual religious tone to their actions and enterprises, frequently disguising their true character, even from themselves.

Ferdinand, unfortunately for his popularity, had nothing of the frank and cordial temper which begets love.

He carried the same cautious and impenetrable frigidity into private life, that he showed in public. "No one," says a writer of the time, "could read his thoughts by any change of his countenance." Calm and calculating, even in trifles, it was too obvious that everything had exclusive reference to self. He seemed to estimate his friends only by the amount of services they could render him. He was not always mindful of these services. Witness his ungenerous treatment of Columbus, the Great Captain, Navarro, Ximenes—the men who shed the brightest luster, and the most substantial benefits, on his reign. Witness also his insensibility to the virtues and long attachment of Isabella, whose memory he could so soon dishonor by a union with one every way unworthy to be her successor.

Ferdinand's connection with Isabella, while it reflected infinite glory on his reign, suggests a contrast most unfavorable to his character. Hers was all magnanimity, disinterestedness, and deep devotion to the interests of her people. His was the spirit of egotism. The circle of his views might be more or less expanded, but self was the steady, unchangeable center. Her heart beat with the generous sympathies of friendship, and the purest constancy to the first, the only object of her love. He, however, indulged in those vices generally sanctioned by the times.

Ferdinand left four natural children, one son and three daughters. The former, Don Alonso de Aragon, was made archbishop of Saragossa when only six years old.

The three daughters were by three different ladies, one of them a noble Portuguese.

Ferdinand was, in short, a shrewd and politic prince, representative of the peculiar genius of the age. While Isabella, discarding all the petty artifices of state policy, and pursuing the noblest ends by the noblest means, stands far above her age.

Imagination took flight in the boundless perspective of the New World; but the results actually realized from the discoveries—at least during the queen's life—were comparatively insignificant. In fact, from financial view, they had been a considerable charge on the crown. This was partly owing to the humanity of Isabella; she interfered, as we have seen, to prevent the compulsory exaction of Indian labor. Subsequently (and immediately after her death, indeed), this was carried to such an extent that nearly half a million of ounces of gold were yearly drawn from the mines of Hispaniola alone. The pearl fishers, and the culture of the sugar cane, introduced from the Canaries, yielded large returns under the same inhumane system.

Ferdinand, who enjoyed, by the queen's testament, half the amount of the Indian revenues, was now fully awakened to their importance. It would be unjust, however, to suppose his views limited to immediate profits. The measures he pursued were, in many respects, well contrived to promote the nobler ends of discovery and colonization. He invited the persons most eminent for nautical science and enterprise—as Pinzon, Solis, Vespucci—to his court, where they constituted a sort of board of navigation, constructing charts, and tracing out new routes for projected voyages. The conduct of this department was intrusted to the last-mentioned navigator, who had the glory—the greatest which accident and caprice ever granted to man—of giving his name to the new hemisphere.

Fleets were now fitted out on a more extended scale, which might vie, indeed, with the splendid equipments of the Portuguese, whose brilliant successes in the east excited the envy of their Castilian rivals. The king occasionally took a share in the voyage, independently of the interest which of right belonged to the crown.

The government, however, realized less from these expensive enterprises than individuals, many of whom, enriched by their official stations, or by accidentally falling in with some hoard of treasure among the savages, returned home to excite the envy of their countrymen. But the spirit of adventure was too high among the Castilians to require much incentive, especially when excluded from its usual field in Africa and Europe.

In this universal excitement, the progress of discovery was pushed forward with a success extraordinary for the times. The winding depths of the Gulf of Mexico were penetrated, as well as the borders of the rich but rugged isthmus, which connects the American continents. In

1512, Florida was discovered by a romantic old knight, Ponce de Leon, who, instead of the magical fountain of health, found his grave there. Solis, another navigator, who had charge of an expedition, projected by Ferdinand, to reach the South Sea by the circumnavigation of the continent, ran down the coast as far as the great Rio de la Plata, where he also was cut off by the savages. In 1513, Vasco Nuñez de Balboa penetrated, with a handful of men, across the narrow part of the Isthmus of Darien, and from the summit of the Cordilleras, the first of Europeans, was greeted with the long-promised vision of the southern ocean.

The news of this event excited a sensation in Spain, inferior only to that caused by the discovery of America. The great object which had so long occupied the imagination of the nautical men of Europe, and formed the purpose of Columbus' last voyage, the discovery of a communication with these far western waters, was now accomplished. The famous spice islands, from which the Portuguese had drawn such countless wealth, were scattered over this sea; and the Castilians, after a journey of a few leagues, might launch their barks on its quiet bosom, and reach, and perhaps claim, the coveted possessions of their rivals, as falling west of the papal line of demarcation. Such were the dreams, and such the actual progress of discovery, at the close of Ferdinand's reign.

I have elsewhere examined the policy pursued by the Catholic sovereigns in the government of their colonies.

The supply of precious metals yielded by them eventually proved far greater than had ever entered into the conception of the most sanguine of the early discoverers. Their prolific soil and genial climate, moreover, afforded an infinite variety of vegetable products, which might have furnished an unlimited commerce with the mother country. Under a judicious protection, their population and productions, steadily increasing, would have enlarged to an incalculable extent the general resources of the empire. Such, indeed, might have been the result of a wise system of legislation.

But the true principles of colonial policy were sadly misunderstood in the sixteenth century. The discovery of a world was estimated, like that of a rich mine, by the value of its returns in gold and silver. Much of Isabella's legislation, it is true, shows that she looked to higher and far nobler objects. But with much that is good, there was mingled, as in most of her institutions, one germ of evil which eventually overshadowed and blighted all the rest. This was the spirit of restriction and monopoly, aggravated by the subsequent laws of Ferdinand, and carried to an extent under the Austrian dynasty, that paralyzed colonial trade.

Under this ingeniously perverse system of laws, the interests of both the parent country and the colonies were sacrificed. The latter, condemned to look for supplies to an incompetent source, were miserably dwarfed in their growth; while the former contrived to convert the nutriment which she extorted from the colonies into a fatal poison. The streams of wealth which flowed in from the silver quarries of Zacatecas and Potosí, were jealously locked up within the limits of the Peninsula.

The great problem, proposed by the Spanish legislation of the sixteenth century, was the reduction of prices in the kingdom to the same level as in other European nations. Every law that was passed, however, tended, by its restrictive character, to augment the evil. The golden tide, which, permitted a free vent, would have fertilized the region through which it poured, now buried the land under a deluge which blighted every green and living thing. Agriculture, commerce, manufactures, every branch of national industry and improvement, languished and fell to decay; and the nation, like the Phrygian monarch, who turned all that he touched to gold, cursed by the very consummation of its wishes, was poor in the midst of its treasures.

Our admiration of the dauntless heroism displayed by the early Spanish navigators is much qualified by a consideration of the cruelties with which it was tarnished. As long as Isabella lived, the Indians found an efficient friend and protector; but "her death," says the venerable Las Casas, "was the signal for their destruction." Immediately on that event, the system of *repartimientos*, originally authorized, as we have seen, by Columbus (who seems to have had no doubt, from the first, of the crown's absolute right of property over the natives) was carried to its full extent in the colonies. Every Spaniard, however humble, had his proportion of slaves; and men, many of them not only incapable of estimating the awful responsibility of the situation, but without the least touch of humanity in their natures, were individually intrusted with the unlimited disposal of the lives and destinies of their fellow-creatures. They abused this trust in the grossest manner; tasking the unfortunate Indian far beyond his strength, inflicting the most refined punishments on the indolent, and hunting down those who resisted or escaped, like so many beasts of chase, with ferocious bloodhounds.

Every step of the white man's progress in the New World, may be said to have been on the corpse of a native. Faith is staggered by the recital of the number of victims immolated in these fair regions within a very few years after the discovery; and the heart sickens at the loathsome details of barbarities, recorded by the friar Bartolomé de Las Casas, who, if his sympathies have led him sometimes to overcolor, can never be suspected of willfully misstating facts of which he was an eyewitness. A selfish indifference to the rights of the original occupants of the soil, is a sin which lies at the door of most of the primitive European settlers, whether papist or puritan, of the New World.

It may seem strange, that no relief was afforded by the government to these oppressed subjects. But Ferdinand, if we may credit Las Casas, was never permitted to know the extent of the injuries done to them. He was surrounded by men in the management of the Indian department, whose interest it was to keep him in ignorance. The remonstrances of some zealous missionaries led him, in 1501, to refer the subject of the *repartimientos* to a council of jurists and theologians. This body yielded to the representations of the advocates of the system, that it was indispensable for maintaining the colonies, since the European was altogether unequal to labor in this tropical climate; and that it, moreover, afforded the only chance for the conversion of the Indian, who, unless compelled, could never be brought in contact with the white man.

On these grounds, Ferdinand openly assumed for himself and his ministers the responsibility of maintaining this vicious institution. He subsequently issued an ordinance to that effect, accompanied, however, by a variety of humane and equitable regulations for restraining its abuse. The license was embraced in its full extent; the regulations were openly disregarded.

Several years after, in 1515, Las Casas, moved by the spectacle of human suffering, returned to Spain, and pleaded the cause of the injured native, in tones which made the dying monarch tremble on his throne. It was too late, however, for the king to execute the remedial measures he contemplated. The efficient interference of Ximenes, who sent a commission for the purpose to Hispaniola, was attended with no permanent results. And the indefatigable "protector of the Indians" was left to sue for redress at the court of Charles,* and to furnish a splendid, if not a solitary example there, of a bosom penetrated with the true spirit of Christian philanthropy.

* Charles I (1500-1558), son of Joanna and Philip. Through his Habsburg connections, he also became Charles V, Holy Roman Emperor (1520), and began the Austrian dominance in Spain. [Editor]

INDEX